Painting Outdoors

RALPH FABRI

PAINTING OUTDOORS

WATSON-GUPTILL PUBLICATIONS, New York

*This book is dedicated to artists and art students
who not only love nature in all her forms and moods,
but also find inspiration in what man has added to
nature: shacks and castles, villages and cities, ships
and carriages, derricks and market places, and the immense
variety of people and their garbs.*

© Copyright 1969 by Ralph Fabri
Published by Watson-Guptill Publications, New York, New York
All Rights Reserved.
Manufactured in U.S.A.
Library of Congress Catalog Card Number: 69-12493

Contents

Acknowledgments

MY EDITORS, Donald Holden and Susan E. Meyer, have given me the most important help I needed: the freedom to write as much on the vast subject of outdoor painting as I wanted to, before they would discuss the length of the book. Their comments and suggestions enabled me to write a truly comprehensive and comprehensible book. Jim Craig put text and illustrations into a most attractive as well as readable shape.

I also wish to thank The Metropolitan Museum of Art, The Thannhauser Foundation, New York, and The National Academy of Design for having graciously lent reproductions of great outdoor paintings in their collections.

Introduction

THERE'S NO END to the variety of outdoor painting. The ramifications, problems, techniques, possibilities of, and approaches to, this subject are truly fantastic. The aim of this book is to help you cope with all this by giving you all imaginable information on the entire subject.

What is outdoor painting?

In the broadest sense, everything outside your house is outdoors. You needn't even leave your home, just look out your window, and there's the outdoors. What you see depends upon your location. It may be the other side of a narrow street, the backyard of your neighbor's house; a park, a lake, a sea, a river; hills, mountains, a forest, a valley, a prairie or a desert, because people live on the edge of the Sahara, too. It's all outdoors.

Division of outdoor subjects

We usually divide the theme into landscapes or scenery; marines or seascapes, and cityscapes. The word "scape" indicates a wide view. It's probably safe to state that the vast majority of outdoor paintings are combinations of two or more elements—a fishing village on the seashore, meadows and forests leading toward mountains; a city park with houses in the background, and the like.

Who paints what and why?

For most city-dwellers, landscape means nature in all her glory, unpolluted air, in a variety of seasons. Artists of the Hudson River School dedicated themselves to the depiction of pure, rustic scenery, and many present-day artists still do that. Cityscape, however, is just as attractive, because even the biggest metropolis offers a combination of natural beauty and man-made magnificence. A quaint old town with its church on a hilltop in Europe; a romantic castle on the Rhine or in Scotland; an American city with its variety of buildings; a village on a poetic river; houses on a lakeshore, reflected in the calm water, all serve as inspiration for artists.

There's the eternal fascination of the sea, the pounding of waves on the rocks, fantastic cloud formations, gliding seagulls, graceful boats, shabby wharves. Many an artist devotes his whole career to just one or the other of these subjects.

Desire for variety or novelty

For the artist who lives near the sea, mountains offer something new. For Northerners, accustomed to snow, there's the attraction of tropical scenery, while artists living in warm climates are stimulated by snow-clad mountains. Plant life itself is an inexhaustible storehouse of themes.

Where do we start?

Accustomed as most of us are to painting indoors, first in classrooms, later in our own studios (or linoleum-floored kitchens), doing mostly still lifes and figures, we don't even know how to start an outdoor painting, which has rules and problems of its own. The chances are that you'll make plenty of mistakes if you do outdoor painting without enough fundamental knowledge. Such mistakes are costly in effort, time, patience, and disappointment. As a matter of fact, there's probably no subject in which a lack of experience is as quickly felt as in outdoor painting.

Talent and skill

Natural talent is something with which you are born, and we assume that anyone wishing to paint has such natural ability. But even the greatest genius has to acquire knowledge and skill. This book will lead you all the way from tools and materials needed in each major pictorial medium to the choosing of your outdoor subject and the selection of the medium best suited to you and to your subject. It will give you full information on sketching, composition, perspective, color mixing and techniques.

It will help you avoid pitfalls in rendering light and shadow, atmospheric effects, reflections in water or in windows; it will teach you how to paint figures, vehicles and other accessories in your outdoor subjects. With the help of step-by-step demonstrations, you'll learn how to start even the most complicated scape on the spot, and finish it in the comfort of your studio.

Painting outdoors is a good habit

Not so very long ago, people believed that the night air was dangerous and that all epidemics were spread merely by the air. Today it's normal to go outdoors, to go on hikes, picnics, to go mountainclimbing, and so forth. We have cars, buses, bicycles, besides trains and planes, for transportation. One can sketch practically all over the world.

Turner used to walk up to twenty-five miles a day, even when he could afford a horse-and-buggy. Probably few of us like to walk so much, but a mile or so is recommended by all physicians. And, as I mentioned before, outdoors is a very comprehensive term. Outdoors can be right in front of your gate, just around the corner, or at a short walking distance. Outdoor painting is good for your health as well as for your art.

Techniques and tools aren't everything

True painting can never be merely a matter of technical know-how. It's deeply involved with esthetic concepts, both modern and traditional. A watch movement can only be put together in one way, if it is to work. All the pieces are there for the skilled worker. In art, the main factors may be the same, but there are innumerable ways of putting them together. This book combines technical advice with artistic and esthetic ideas.

1 Historical background

PLINY, OR, TO USE HIS FULL NAME, Gaius Plinius Secundus the Elder, who lived from A.D. 23 to 79, was a Roman naturalist, encyclopedist and writer, whose knowledge and experience were among the finest in classic times. In his still widely-read writings, he highly praised Ludius, or Studius, a painter of the Augustan period. This painter had introduced a style of wall decorations in which "villas, harbors, landscape, gardens, sacred groves, woods, hills, fishponds, straits, streams and shores, any scene in short that took his fancy, were depicted in lively and facile fashion."

Pompeiian murals include many such scenes; we find similar subjects done in low relief, made of stucco, in the Cretan manner, in murals around the Villa Farnesina, now in the Museo delle Terme, in Rome. Pictures of a garden, executed on the four walls of a room in the Villa Livia at Prima Porta, near Rome, are the most splendid examples of landscape, especially trees, in classic Western art. It's quite possible that these were created by the artist so prominently singled out by Pliny. Pompeiian murals representing events from the *Odyssey* always emphasize the scenery, even though large figures are shown in the foreground. As a matter of fact, the aim of Pompeiian artists was to open up the walls of very small rooms, thus making them look bigger, airier, by painting outdoor pictures with large vistas in vivid, realistic colors.

Outdoor pictures in the Middle Ages

In the Middle Ages, landscape was barely more than symbolic. Churches, castles, single trees, rocks, perhaps clouds, represented the outdoors. Figures from the Bible were of much more significance. It wasn't until the early fifteenth century that the beginnings of landscape painting appeared. Masaccio (1401–1428), so important an artist in many respects, seems to have led the way in this field as well. Nevertheless, landscape remained subordinate to figures, and was usually conventionalized, naively distorted, even though its details were more accurately observed.

First mountain scenery

Tiziano Vecelli (1477–1576), the name anglicized into Titian, was the first artist to paint mountains with real knowledge and love, probably because he was mountain-bred. Venetian artists were generally the first to give a feeling of spaciousness in their scenic backgrounds, perhaps because their fabulous city was so restricted in space. Flemish and other northern artists were more interested in minute details. Albrecht Dürer (1472–1528), with his German goldsmith ancestry and training, followed this cold style, but he is believed to have been the first Western artist to paint landscapes and cityscapes in watercolor from direct observation. Dürer used these sketches as backgrounds for figure compositions in his paintings and graphic arts, but his outdoor sketches stand out as individual works of art.

Classicist landscape

In southern Europe, the Italian artist, Salvator Rosa (1615–1673), was more interested in romantic and picturesque scenery. The so-called classicist landscape was largely developed in Italy in the seventeenth century. Everything was idealized in these pictures. French artists soon adopted this style. Claude Lorrain (Gelée), and Nicholas Poussin filled such landscapes with mythological or semi-historical figures. Artists of the Netherlands, however, displayed the stronger sense of ordinary, everyday realism characteristic of their part of Europe.

Topography and art

Long before landscape became a subject for artists, topographers often made charming or artistic renderings of a particular area, usually for the owners of the land. Such drawings, occasionally turned into engravings or woodcuts, emphasized detail and usually tried to make places look more impressive than they really were. Joseph Mallord William Turner (1775–1851), started out as a topographer. He loved the outdoors and was one of the first artists working outdoors, from direct observation. His fellow-countryman, John Constable (1776–1837), was another pioneer in this field. He painted literally hundreds of small pictures on the spot, rather than from imagination the way classicist landscape painters had done. Turner and Constable are considered the fathers of Impressionism.

Outdoor painting in Oriental art

Nature worship seems to have been the foundation of spiritual life in the Far East. In Oriental art, man is exactly as much a part of nature as a tree, a rock, a mountain, a cricket, a bird, a house, a footbridge, or a fly. No more and no less. An imitation of Chinese art became fashionable in Western European furniture and furnishings during the eighteenth century. Called *chinoiserie*, this furniture borrowed figures, birds, floral ornaments, clouds, and other elements from Chinese articles which had reached the West through tradesmen. But Oriental art had no effect on Occidental fine art until quite recent times.

It was the historic opening of Japan by Commodore Matthew Calbraith Perry in 1853 that started the spreading of Japanese woodcuts, painted scrolls, and other Oriental art objects all over Europe. The non-photographic, yet fully recognizable Japanese pictures inspired Western artists who were just then faced with the camera, a creation of the machine age. Many people thought the camera would make hand-painted pictures obsolete. Artists were desperately looking for effects the camera could not achieve, instead of trying to be as accurate as possible.

A new look in outdoor painting

Japanese paintings and woodcuts undoubtedly contributed to the fast development of Impressionism, a new way of looking at things. No longer was it necessary to depict every tiny detail. The idea was to paint one's impression, the essence of what one saw. Impressionism, above all, was outdoor painting to a large extent.

American landscape painting

The first American development in art was the Hudson River School, whose artists depicted nature in her most romantic, most enchanting, most rustic state, untouched, therefore unspoiled by human hands. It was too beautiful for words, but strictly realistic, executed from keen observation.

By the end of the nineteenth century, however, more and more American artists went to France to study painting, as France had become the center of new-fangled art. Many American artists, George Inness, for example, returned with the ideals of Impressionism. In 1913, the Armory Show in New York introduced "modern" art to the New World. Gertrude Vanderbilt Whitney opened a gallery for artists trying to express themselves in unorthodox ways.

Marines or seascapes

Roman artists depicted the sea in paintings and mosaics with great skill, usually enriching such scenes with remarkably accurate pictures of denizens of the sea. Roman artists also found it interesting to show bikini-clad bathing beauties on the seashore. As a motif for painters, seascapes were also popular in seventeenth century Holland. With these two exceptions, however, the sea used to serve only as location for biblical, historical, or mythological events, until recent times, when vacationing by the sea became fashionable. In the United States, Winslow Homer popularized seascape painting with his powerful aquarelles and oils. Turner's dramatic pictures of the sea, painted in the first half of the nineteenth century, didn't become famous until long after his death.

Cityscapes

Ancient Egyptian coffins, mummy cases often had representations of streets; wall paintings in tombs often included houses and silos, as a symbol of eternal life in the hereafter. The houses were drawn in a diagrammatic style, just like all other subjects in Egyptian art. Frescoes in Cretan palaces give an adequate idea of the gaily-colored architecture in a civilization which preceded Greek civilization by many centuries. Ancient Greek painting is dedicated largely to figures. The Romans, on the other hand, loved all kinds of city and harbor scenes, depicting watertowers, bridges, temples, and other buildings in a perfectly recognizable manner. As a rule, though, the city served as a background for mythological or historical figures and events.

Landscape (left) by Asher B. Durand (American, 1796–1886), a leader of the Hudson River School, and one of the first fifteen founders of the National Academy of Design, New York, 1825. Asymmetrical composition is preferred ever since the Baroque period. Every detail in this painting is carefully done, but there's a fine sense of distance. This is achieved by delicate, soft colors in the distance, as well as by the larger sizes of trees and rocks in the foreground. Collection National Academy of Design.

Entrance to a Village (above) by Meindert Hobbema (Dutch, 1638–1709), oil on wood 29½″ x 43⅜″. Artists of the Netherlands loved to depict the tiniest detail, but not to the detriment of the over-all picture. This scene is viewed from the level of the road as you approach the village, not from a hilltop. The dirt road leads your eyes far into the distance, not upward. Bequest of Benjamin Altman, 1913, The Metropolitan Museum of Art.

View of Toledo by El Greco (Spanish, 1541–1614), oil on canvas 47¾" x 42"; signed in Greek "Domenicos Theotocopoulos made it." By the time El Greco painted this famous atmospheric landscape, the symmetry of the Renaissance had given way to an off-centered presentation. El Greco was too temperamental for small details, and he had the inclination to make towers and buildings as well as figures more slender than they were in reality. The ominous sky is one of the most celebrated features of this painting. It is probably the artist's subconscious reaction to the Inquisition. Bequest of Mrs. H. O. Havemeyer, 1929. The H. O. Havemeyer Collection, The Metropolitan Museum of Art.

16

Cityscapes in the Christian era

Early Christian artists continued the Roman custom of painting figures with architectural backdrops. Churches and palaces were usually identifiable, but cities were almost always of an imaginary nature even after the Dark Ages. Artists of the Renaissance still had quaint notions about Jerusalem, Thebes, Constantinople (Istanbul), and other famed ancient cities often included in their paintings.

In an age when travel was a dangerous adventure, artists knew only the cities and countrysides in which they were living. A few artists worked in several cities. Canaletto, for example, painted London as well as Venice, but most artists never had the opportunity to see something really different. They only heard of fabulous foreign places. As a result, biblical cities were painted like German cities by German artists; like French towns by French artists; like Flemish cities by artists of Flanders. *Feast in the House of Levy,* a magnificent painting by Paolo Veronese (1528–1588), is a typical mixture of a Roman palace with carved figures; a background of Gothic and Renaissance buildings; people dressed according to the period of the artist, not in the time when Jesus dined at the house of Levy. In his *Assumption of the Virgin,* El Greco (1541–1614) shows the Holy Virgin ascending to heaven directly from the City of Toledo, where the Cretan-born Spanish artist was living and working.

Impressionism versus classicism

After a period of painstaking renderings in the classicist period, the Impressionists took up cityscapes with great enthusiasm, because the subject was just around the corner. They could also easily prove their contention that colors are constantly changing—they painted the same view in the morning and in the afternoon, on a rainy day and on a sunny day, in various seasons. They also added pedestrian and vehicular traffic as they saw it from a distance, in motion or standing still, and always as parts of the entire picture, not as if figures and vehicles were of any particular significance.

Post-Impressionist cityscapes

The same changes occurred in the depiction of cities as in other subjects of painting. Hardly did Impressionism spread over Europe and America when Futurism, Cubism, Abstraction, Dada, and other "schools" of art came in rapid succession, overlapping each other. Kandinsky, Matisse, Braque, Picasso, Mondrian, Kokoschka, Klee, Arp, and other now world-famous artists went through many changes in style, going from the academic to the abstract and the nonobjective. Of course, there's no such thing as a nonobjective cityscape. Nonobjective implies a total lack of any factual subject matter. But an abstract cityscape is quite possible.

Today, cityscapes are as many-faceted as other subjects. An artist can paint a very realistic view of a city and make it highly individual in color and composition. Photographic fidelity in all details is not required.

La Grenouillière (The Frog Pond) by Claude Monet (French, 1840–1926), oil on canvas 29⅜″ x 34¼″. One of Monet's paintings was the basis of the name "Impressionism." Although very different in technique from paintings done in previous times, the fundamental composition is as off-centered as the works of Dutch and Hudson River School painters. Note the boldly applied ripples and reflections in the water; they appear to be in actual motion. Bequest of Mrs. H. O. Havemeyer, 1929. The H. O. Havemeyer Collection, The Metropolitan Museum of Art.

2 Equipment for outdoor painting

IN YOUR STUDIO, you can draw and paint whenever you feel like it or have the time. You have all tools and materials on hand; you're normally safe and comfortable; you can disconnect your telephone if you don't want to be disturbed. You can stop any time, and start again when you're ready for it.

Outdoor painting requires planning

For outdoor work, you need mental as well as physical equipment. You have to consider the weather, the necessity of staying outdoors for a certain (or uncertain) length of time. Make sure to take with you everything you would possibly need. At the same time, you don't want to burden yourself with superfluous items. Tools and materials will be listed separately for each medium, in the respective chapters. Here, I'll talk about outdoor equipment in general.

Consider the weather

You're unlikely to go outdoors to paint in dreadful weather, but it's possible to paint a hurricane or blizzard through a window, in a comfortable room. I know a New England artist specializing in snowscapes, who's built a studio on wheels: a steel-and-glass booth on the chassis of an old automobile. This moving atelier is properly heated; the artist can stop anywhere and paint snow scenes from actual observation.

The same idea would work in a tropical country, with an air-conditioned studio on wheels. One might spend an artistically exciting and valuable period in the National Parks of South Africa or in the jungles of the Amazon, driving around in places where normally no artist could paint pictures. Give this idea a thought.

Drive or walk?

Unless you wish to emulate Turner and walk twenty-five miles a day, and unless you live in a place where interesting views exist all round, you'll have to go to your outdoor subject by car, bicycle, train or bus; and, in all likelihood, you'll have to walk around a bit until you find a satisfactory spot to paint.

What to wear

A well-dressed person wears garments appropriate for the occasion. Consider the place where you're going: will there be tall weeds, underbrush, stones, rough terrain, perhaps poison ivy, or plenty of dust? Wear the right kind of shoes, comfortable dress or suit, slacks, rather than a skirt, if you're a woman; warm clothing if it isn't very warm or if you think the weather will turn cool by the time you finish your painting. Remember that, even on a very pleasant day, you might feel chilly if you stand or sit in one spot for hours.

What about snakes?

Believe me, I have no desire to frighten you out of painting in the country, but you ought to inquire about snakes. You may find that there are snakes, but all of them non-poisonous. I've seen more than once how horrified city people were at the sight of such a non-poisonous, beneficial snake coiling across a rock twenty feet away. I also recall the time when I happily walked around a beautiful section of the Carpathian Mountains, enjoying the sight and ready to make a few sketches, until I met a forester, who stopped me with an exclamation of astonishment: "What are you doing here without a cane and without wearing leggings or boots? Don't you know that this is viper country?" No, I didn't know. I thanked him and walked back to my hotel as fast as I could, seeing vipers all over the place.

What about sunburn?

It's one thing to take a sunbath on your roof or on the beach—where you apply suntan oil to your exposed body—and another thing to be engrossed in painting and being burnt to the bone without realizing it until it really hurts. Even if the sun seems to be hidden behind clouds, you can get a severe sunburn. Use common sense: cover your legs and arms, and your head. Wear a broad-brimmed hat or a kerchief on your head and on the nape of your neck.

Food and drink

If you expect to stay out long, in a place far from even a roadside food and drink stand, carry food and water, coffee or tea in thermos bottles or boxes. Don't count on taking a little time out from painting, and driving to a place where you find something to eat. You cannot leave your equipment in the wilderness; once you stop working, you might as well pack up and call it a day.

How long are you going to work?

The length of time you work depends upon the size of your support, the complex or simple nature of your subject, and how fast you paint. The season is also a factor. The days are long in the summer, but shorter in the spring and fall. (The problem of changing lights and shadows will be discussed in a special chapter.) Suffice it now to say that you can hardly work on the same picture for more than two or three hours in midsummer, and probably not longer than an hour and a half on shorter days.

To sit or to stand?

Whatever your medium, and whether you like to sit or to stand, a folding stool should always be carried on an outdoor painting trip. It should be large enough for comfort and safety. Small ones have a habit of toppling over, without warning; they may dump paint in your lap, and dump you into your paintbox or into the weed. Even if you work in a standing position, the stool is a good place for your palette, brushes, and other items.

Easel for outdoors

A so-called French folding easel, which contains an ingeniously built-in paintbox, is fine for oils and polymer. For transparent watercolor and wet casein, a tripod with a tiltable board is available, but many aquarellists work on a hardcover block which they can hold in their laps, sitting on a stool, with paintbox and water jar on the ground. Felt brush sketching can be done in a standing or sitting position, but the support must be held horizontally or at a slight slant. One cannot work with felt brush or ball-point pen on a support kept vertically, because the nib has to be pressed downward in order to show results.

Aluminum folding easels are quite sturdy and easy to push into the soil. Whatever easel or other contraption you acquire, try it out at home before going outdoors. Don't take it for granted that you know how to handle it. I've seen inexperienced artists getting into a rage, ending up in total frustration, by attempting to find out which part of a folding gadget serves what purpose.

Supports for outdoors

Very large supports are hard to carry, and you have to consider the fact that any support might suddenly act like a sail. A breeze can hurtle it away, perhaps carrying the easel, and even the artist, with it. Canvas on stretchers sails faster than anything else and is likely to be torn as it flies into a tree or onto the ground. Boards caught by a gust of wind are likely to end up with a corner or two broken. I wouldn't try to take a support bigger than about 25″ x 30″, and would handle it with care. I'd find out the direction of the wind before placing the support on the easel.

I am trying to warn you of all these little possibilities in order to save you from disagreeable experiences. You have to be more alert outdoors than indoors. When your work is finished, at least for the day, you have to be even more careful in handling the support, especially if it's an oil painting. Any support with an oil painting may fall on its face, just like buttered bread, if you drop it.

Water! water!

If you work in any of the water media—aquarelle, casein, polymer—make sure to carry enough water, unless you're absolutely sure you can obtain clean, fresh water on location. There are container-and-cup combinations, but these hold very little water and, after a while, they become rusty and discolor the water. Carry water in bottles. Remember, too, that brushes have to be washed immediately after being used in casein or polymer. It's better to have too much water than not enough.

How to keep your things together

Your best bet is to carry a dropcloth, the kind of muslin used by house-painters on the floor, or any other solid-colored textile strong enough to hold your supplies. I once saw a young student roll out a lovely piece of chintz, decorated with floral designs in natural colors. It was a nightmare to look for paints, brushes, or caps of tubes on it. On a solid-colored material, you can see what's what. At the end, you can pull the corners together and tie everything into a bundle.

Umbrellas for artists

Many of the Impressionists used an umbrella outdoors. Winston S. Churchill had a butler carrying a beach umbrella whenever he painted outdoors. Most of us have no butlers, and an umbrella for outdoor painting can be a nuisance. It adds weight to your art load, and it's difficult to set it up. I prefer to wear a broad-brimmed hat, such as a coolie strawhat, and to turn or move easel and support, if necessary, to get out of the sun.

Keep the sun off your support

Most supports are white, and even if you give your support a tone, the sun hitting it can be blinding. Colors applied to a sunlit support look much brighter than they are in normal light, so that your sense of color is bound to be impaired while, at the same time, your eyes are being damaged. When working under a tree, the shadows of the foliage are uneven: with bright sunspots in between. This causes some parts of your painting to look bright, other parts to look grayish-blue. And the breeze invariably rustles the leaves and thus causes endless motion on your support. Make sure to have the same light all over the support, and no sunlight. There's always a possibility of tilting the support or turning it in a slightly different direction, in order to eliminate lights and shadows on it.

Avoid working in a position that causes the shadow of your head and shoulders to fall on the support. I've found that most beginners fail to realize the consequences, physical and artistic, of this exposure of the support to the vagaries of sunlight and shadow. On a number of occasions, students tried to wear sunglasses. They didn't believe that sunglasses change all colors, until I showed them how the scenery seen through the polaroid glass looked entirely different from the same scenery viewed with the naked eye.

It's also of great importance not to look at brilliantly sunlit parts of the subject too long at a time, because this causes you to see jumping, dancing purple, green and blue or red spots.

Who likes insects?

Entomologists like insects, not artists working outdoors! Flies, gnats, mosquitoes and other ubiquitous flying creatures are a nuisance. Sprays are available now to keep insects away for hours at a time. Take such a spray with you and use it on yourself, your equipment, your support. Whether they are art-lovers or not, insects do like to crawl all over your painting, and get stuck in the wet paint. You can scrape them off, or cover them up, in an oil or polymer painting, but how about a watercolor or casein? You'll have to scrape off the paint as well as the insects.

What about a rainy day?

A rainy day is often attractive from an artistic viewpoint, as it gives everything a soft, grayish tint, without any harsh contrasts. Rain doesn't affect oil colors, but may damage the support and, certainly, you shouldn't stand or sit in the rain or drizzle. Water media are impossible to use in the rain. You might paint a rainy scene from under a roof or some other cover, such as the interior of a station wagon. Don't risk your health by getting soaking wet.

What about people?

A kind of diplomacy is required in dealing with local people. You cannot simply disregard their existence. Whenever I work outdoors, on private property, near a house, shack or farm, I introduce myself to the nearest human being and ask for permission to depict his property. In European countries, people are accustomed to artists. The only time you have to ask permission is when you actually invade a picturesque courtyard or private garden. In the United States, however, the custom is not so wide-spread, and you never know when somebody will resent any intrusion.

I had a painful experience in a small Pennsylvania town many years ago. Opening my folding stool, I sat down to sketch a charming little church on Main Street. Several passers-by looked on for a while. Suddenly, a minister appeared and challenged me. What was I doing there? Who had given me permission to sketch that church? When I stated that I didn't think any permission was necessary to sketch a public building, he said the church wasn't a public building, it was a private church, and he threatened to have me arrested.

I tore up my sketch, folded my chair, bowed to the minister, and walked to a drugstore right behind me. I bought a postcard with the picture of the church on it; waved it at the minister who was still there, manifestly trying to inform the group which had gathered that I had attempted to do something illegal, if not diabolical. I am sure this was an extreme case, but I have learnt my lesson.

It's an undeniable fact that artists would rather paint dilapidated, ramshackle places, with broken window panes, unworkable doors, peeling paint, patched-up roofs, cracked walls, than beautiful new houses. It's hard to explain to the owner or tenant of a decrepit place that you aren't trying to make fun of his property; that you're not planning any propaganda; that you're inspired by the picturesque beauty of his place. You have to make a real effort at talking to such people. At the end, they might even think that, after all, their place is not so bad.

What can you do when you're not wanted somewhere? Call the Civil Liberties Union? Some people are sensitive, rather than sensible. Arguing with them is hopeless. Go away and look for a more receptive neighborhood. On the other hand, local people may be friendly and watch you, addressing to you some of the silliest questions you'd ever heard. Well, consider the questions you might ask a farmer. Wouldn't they be silly, too?

Watch out for taboos

There are religious and social taboos of all kinds. Try to find out about them, especially before you paint in a foreign country. In some places, local people consider painting on a Sunday or on a Saturday irreligious. Despite neon lights, huge Cadillacs, resplendent hotels and restaurants, Muslim communities still often object to any depiction of humans and animals, although they don't seem to object to the taking of photographs of the same subjects.

Many Japanese still bathe nude; women and men bathe together in countless places, in a complete disregard for Western customs. You'll find such places in the center of many a town. Women in some Latin American countries do their laundering at creeks or lakes, naked from the waist up. This doesn't mean, though, that these Japanese or Latin Americans would allow you to paint pictures of them. They'd probably chase you out of town if you ever tried.

This is also true for peasant women who breast-feed their babies in public, sitting on a bench, a stoop or a stone. If you're interested in depicting such native figures, take snapshots or make quick sketches in an unobtrusive manner. Avoid hurting the feelings of strangers. It's bad enough to hurt the feelings of friends.

3 How to select your subject

WHAT MARVELOUS COLORS! Look at those beautiful mountains! Isn't it like a dream? Something out of a fairy tale! These and similar exclamations are made by millions of people first beholding some of the great beauty spots of this globe. Many people also add that they wish they were artists, so that they could depict such views in all their glory.

Views for laymen

Nowadays, few people travel without cameras, and even the least experienced person is bound to find a couple of excellent snapshots among the scores he had taken. You can photograph the entire scenery, all round, by moving your camera a few degrees left or right after every shot, and then pasting the developed pictures next to each other.

Views for artists

An artist cannot paint scores of pictures without sacrificing much time, energy, materials and actual labor. It's one thing to snap a photograph, and another thing to paint the same picture on a small support. The artist has to select a view which will give an idea of the whole scenery, even though showing only a very small part of it. A view may look magnificent as your eyes move up and down, right and left; yet, many individual sections of it may appear quite dull.

How about a view finder?

Nobody would dream of taking a photograph without looking at the subject through the view finder which is part of every camera. Why not use a view finder in painting? The Impressionists often used a reducing mirror in which they could judge the final picture better than they could by looking at the real scenery. Or they turned one hand into a sort of looking glass by forming a squarish hole with their fingers, the tip of the thumb touching the tip of the index finger. Looking through this hole with one eye, the other eye closed, they would find the most artistic view.

Still others made a view finder by cutting a small, oblong hole in a piece of cardboard. Holding such a view finder horizontally or vertically, a little closer to one eye, or a little farther away, you can visualize the finished picture. You might go one step further by gluing black threads across the hole, half an inch from each other, horizontally and vertically. Instead of threads, you can cover the hole with transparent acetate and draw the grid lines on it with a ruling pen, in India ink.

Look at scenery through a hole made with your fingers. This enables you to concentrate on one section at a time.

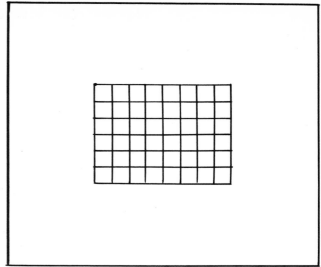

View finder: a piece of cardboard with a 3″ x 4″ rectangular hole covered with clear acetate, gridded with vertical and horizontal lines half an inch apart. As in a camera, the view finder shows you the full picture. The grid also gives you a good idea of proportions and perspective.

Through such a gridded viewer, you can see the proportions and perspective as well as the general effect. This wonderful little gadget would gradually train your eyes to see everything in flat pictures. Albrecht Dürer, and many other Renaissance masters, used a viewer divided into squares. Why not try it?

Selecting a landscape

In landscape painting, features of the earth and nature predominate, but houses, and often people, may be involved. Perhaps more than anything else, a good landscape has to have a kind of pattern which attracts the eye. You cannot merely pile up trees, bushes, rocks and so forth. A visible design of hills, road, trees, etc. should be the foundation upon which you develop details.

Look around first

Frame the different sections of your scene with your view finder or your fingers, until you find a particular section which appeals to you more than the rest. In all likelihood, no part will be perfect. Here's where the artist comes in. He can do what the most expensive camera cannot achieve: he can use his taste, judgment, and creative ability. Select the best over-all view; take items from other parts, and telescope them into one picture. Your painting will still be as realistic as you wish to make it, even if it isn't an exact replica of nature.

Light and shadow

The same scenery looks quite different in different lights, under various atmospheric conditions. Select a section in which the light-and-shadow effect seems just right, but choose another part of the scenery, in which the pattern is more inspiring, and render it in the light you prefer. This is by no means as simple as it sounds, and I suggest that, at first, you paint the light-and-shadow effect just as it happens to be, but think of the other possibility later. Telescoping some small items, such as a cluster of trees, or an unusual rock formation, doesn't alter the atmospheric mood of a painting.

Selecting marines or seascapes

Water of some sort is the main feature of seascapes, but there are countless items which can be included. Beaches, rocks, dunes, islands; trees, boats of innumerable kinds; wharves, docks, shipyards, fishing gear, shacks, fishermen, sailors; sea gulls, flying or standing still. As a matter of fact, marine painting is a vast field in itself, which demands concentrated study, besides a very special love for the theme.

This book considers seascapes only as a part of outdoor painting in general. You might paint a lake, a sea, a river on one of your excursions.

Telescoping seascapes

Many artists would paint a single, gracefully curving wave over the whole support. However, most artists like to add the picturesque colorful sights connected with the sea. Here, too, a view finder may be employed to good advantage. Try to select the most characteristic over-all view, then add other items. But avoid any hodge-podge, such as a fishing shack from Bretagne on the Italian Riviera, with pine trees growing out of the dunes, gondolas on Lake Ontario, and the like.

Selecting of cityscapes

A view of any part of a city is a cityscape, even if the picture includes parks, hills, lake, river, forest. Some people abhor cities and call them ugly. Yet, there are many inspiringly beautiful cities, in which natural scenery is combined with man-made masterpieces of architecture and planning in perfect harmony.

It isn't enough to paint houses next to each other, floor upon floor, windows and windows by the dozen, roofs and chimneys. Select the subject according to color, form, a variety of architectural features, in an interesting perspective. You often have a better view from a higher floor than from the sidewalk, and from an angle, rather than from a frontal point of view.

The corner of a square, with a few trees, an unusual intersection, or a group of old houses is a more stimulating subject than even the most staggering steel-and-glass structure. A view finder is a great help in this subject, too. It's especially important to decide how big a part, and what part of a particular building should be in the picture. It isn't necessary to depict the whole house. One section of a colorful structure may be more attractive than a repetition of the same kinds of floors and windows.

Telescoping houses

Unless you're painting a completely historical, well-known place, you're free to make changes for the sake of artistic variety. Move one building nearer, push another one out of the way. But such changes must be made with a full understanding of perspective. You can move a cluster of trees half a mile; no perspective is involved. Trees can be of any shape and size. You cannot replace a one-story house with a ten-story structure without knowing how to draw windows, floors, roof correctly.

You can paint a whole city from a distance. You'll find many picturesque towns nestling in a valley; houses built on hillsides and hilltops. Juneau, the capital of Alaska, has unforgettable natural surroundings; it looks fabulous from a distance, although there probably isn't one single attractive or paintable building in the whole city.

Subject and weather

It isn't enough to select a subject; you have to select the weather as well. On a sunny day, contrasts are strong, lights are bright, shadows well-defined. On a cloudy day, everything is hazy, without sharp differences between light and shadow. It's ideal to have the time to observe a subject in different kinds of weather, at different times of the day, before deciding just when to paint it.

Time of day

In the morning, the sun is yellowish, cool. At noontime, it's a warmer yellow. In the afternoon, it turns more and more reddish. At sunset, the sun is an enormous orange globe. In the morning, the sun is on one side; at noon, it's practically above your head; in the afternoon, it goes lower and lower in the opposite direction. The light-and-shadow effect has surprises for the beginner. A certain subject may look better when the light comes from the upper right and the shadows are on the left, than vice-versa.

Snow, rain, and storm

Snowscapes in sunshine are beautiful and very salable subjects, and can be done outdoors if you're properly dressed. Rain, hurricane, blizzard, and sandstorm can be fascinating subjects, but have to be done from indoors or on the basis of keen observation, after the storm. It's possible to observe a storm from indoors, make a sketch of the colors, and later, make a good drawing for a full-scale painting and paint it on the basis of the sketch.

Sunset, evening, night

Sunset is one of the favorite subjects of outdoor artists. The glorious colors of the sky, reflected or contrasted by the scenery, are a source of inspiration. Evening or twilight effects are usually relaxing. In such subjects, you have to work fast, for short periods of time, because the colors change very quickly. I find it necessary to make a good layout by broad daylight, selecting an interesting subject. Then I go into it with the subtle colors of twilight, or the brilliant tones of a sunset, concentrating on colors and values. You cannot begin to look for the right place, the correct composition while the colors of nature change by the minute.

The same is true in a night scene, be it landscape, seascape, or cityscape. You have to know what you're going to paint before you start applying the colors. These subjects require much acute observation, usually over a period of time. You also have to know how to create certain radiant color effects. The finishing always has to be done from memory, but on the basis of knowledge and observation.

Select colors as well as forms

Colors are important in all subjects, but especially in these so-called "colorful" projects. Nothing is easier than to make a theatrical, flashy picture, full of irrelevant colors. Art should rely on subtlety and experimentation. Try out diverse combinations of color harmonies and color contrasts. Above all, though, keep your eyes open, and observe everything you wish to paint.

Specializing in a subject

Outdoor painting is so vast a realm that one can easily understand why certain artists specialize in one field or another. One artist excels in painting watercolors of French or Italian cityscapes just after a refreshing rain; another artist does oil paintings of nothing but boats and old wharves with sea gulls; still another prefers to do snowscapes in oils; a certain watercolorist paints doorways and public fountains in Mexico. But artists who specialize are no different from medical specialists. They still have to know the same basic facts. Before you can pick your own specialized career, you have to know how to pick it. Try every outdoor subject, in every medium, before you decide to stick to one or the other for the rest of your natural life. Then, you have to study every imaginable phase of your special subject, all its variations.

4 Sketching outdoors

A SKETCH IS A SIMPLY OR ROUGHLY EXECUTED DRAWING OR PAINTING, giving the essential features without details. Or it is a general design or plan for a more complete piece of work. Speed is always implied in sketching. Whether you're making a spontaneous layout for a painting, or jotting down something you see, the sketch has to be done fast, and often in an uncomfortable position. You may notice something unique or bizarre; a strange figure, an interesting or odd group, a seldom-seen old vehicle; a scene you'd like to incorporate in a major painting, and you want to jot it down on a small piece of paper.

A sketch is a kind of shorthand for artists. It may be your own personal shorthand, one you alone can understand, and meaningless to other people. Sketching may be a combination of lines and written notes. Sketching helps you develop a better observing ability by literally compelling you to look and draw fast. It also helps you in coordinating your visual perception with your manual dexterity.

Sketch from various viewpoints

Make sketches from different angles. Go a little higher or lower, left or right, if possible. This will help you see the visual relationship between diverse parts of whatever you're sketching. Above all, it will help you find the most attractive or interesting view. I've seen artists set up their equipment and dash off a painting, only to find out afterwards, much to their chagrin, that the view would have been incomparably better from a spot ten or twelve feet farther.

Study individual objects

Study and draw diverse items from several views, such as a solitary tree, a couple of rocks, a nicely winding road, an old silo, an abandoned, rusting or rotting piece of machinery. Meeting natural, inanimate objects can be the same as meeting people. Stop and find out about them, their personalities, instead of quickly passing them after a glance. For a true artist, meeting and knowing an unusual rock formation or an old tree trunk may be as great a pleasure as meeting some very fine people.

Carry paper and pencil

Since my earliest youth, I never went and never go anywhere without a small sketchbook, or at least a few sheets of paper in my inside pocket, and a ballpoint pen or a pencil, usually a mechanical pencil which needs no sharpening. I'll sketch an acrobatic act in a circus, a graceful step at a ballet, an unusual character in the subway. In Fairbanks, Alaska, I once noticed a very ugly fountain outside the hotel—actually a vertical pipe with water bubbling and jumping out of its mouth. But the splashes of water spurting out of the pipe looked like tiny figures jumping continuously, diving into the concrete basin in all directions, making somersaults, jackknives, and so forth. One day, I'll work it into some fantastic picture.

The purpose of sketches

You accumulate sketches for future inspiration and help. At times when I cannot go outdoors, I peruse my sketches and often find ample material for serious paintings. You have to be careful, of course, not to make a silly, impossible combination of things seen and sketched in various parts of the world. Don't add a colorful house of Hong Kong to a picture of a New England town.

Keep sketches where you can find them

Keep your sketches in sketchbooks or in a portfolio. You might classify them according to subject, and keep them in a sort of alphabetical file. Does it sound funny that an artist might be methodical? It's not a bit funnier than the surgeon who keeps his surgical instruments in so orderly a fashion that he can lay his hand on the required piece almost without looking at it.

Tools and materials for sketching

An 8″ x 10″ or 9″ x 12″ sketchbook of bond paper (typewriter paper), and a pencil or ballpoint pen are the simplest sketching materials. The advantage of the ballpoint pen is that you cannot erase it. This may force you to be more careful, but it also eliminates the notion that a sketch must be perfect and neat. A sketch is perfect if it represents the object in a satisfactory manner. If you make a mistake, go over it with other, perhaps heavier, lines. Always start with the lightest possible lines, so that the stronger lines of the corrections will dominate the finished product.

A dozen colored pencils, sold in a flat box, are another good medium. Such pencils are smudgeproof and give a general idea of the colors in your subject, even though colored pencils or crayons cannot produce truly realistic hues and shades. Felt brush pens work and dry fast on any paper.

Aquarelle sketching

Many aquarellists carry a tiny box of the finest watercolors, with a short-handled brush, a water container with its own cup, and a small block of good watercolor paper. The problem here is that you have to work in a sitting position, because you cannot hold paper and paintbox in one hand while painting with the other. The watercolor sketches of Turner, Constable, and Sargent are often true works of art.

What to look for in sketching

Consider the over-all shape and proportions of any object or scene. Train your eyes to see whether something is wider than high, or higher than wide. You'll be surprised to find how optical illusions can fool you. A tall tree always seems to be higher than wide, yet there are trees in which this isn't the case. A little measuring with your eyes, or with the help of a long pencil, can be of immense help to any artist and any art student.

Panoramic views

When you're trying to sketch a vast scenery, indicate the main pattern of what you see, rather than small details. Cultivated land often forms geometric designs. In the Netherlands, where the land is as flat as a table, the pattern is so geometric that one is inclined to believe it was this severe and precise way of planting in his native country that inspired Piet Mondrian to develop his purely geometric paintings, made up of horizontal and vertical stripes.

On a hilly terrain, you often find a wavy pattern running uphill or downhill, perhaps converging into a bend in a road. In mountainous country, where every fertile spot has to be utilized, spiraling or step-like patterns dominate the view and, very often, terraces are constructed for planting, as in Japan, the Philippines, and the Andes region. Once the main design is caught in your sketch, add details.

Man-made objects

Houses, shacks, churches are normally parts of scenery. Sketch such items with emphasis on their proportions and perspective; that is, the way they appear to your eye. Full explanation of perspective will be found in a separate chapter. All I want to say here is that you should forget the frontal aspect of a building and draw what you see from where you are looking.

Mountains and hills

It seems that a great many art students think of mountains as big camels' humps, and they visualize hills as almost uniform waves of the sea. Such stylized forms are fine in heraldry. In the fine arts, you have to observe the variety in shapes and sizes. No two hills or mountain peaks are ever exactly alike. Look at the main proportions, the silhouettes of faraway hills; compare heights and widths. See which hill is in front, which is in the rear.

Rock formations

Rocks also come in a tremendous variety of forms, sizes, and colors. Rocks exposed to water—rain, river, lake, or ocean—have rounded corners; rocks obtained by blasting have ragged edges and corners. You needn't draw every crevice, every crack, but indicate the bigger planes, breaks, and proportions of such natural objects.

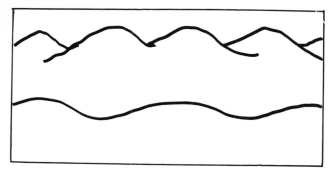

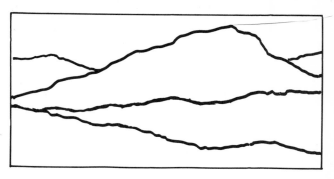

The popular idea of mountains and hills: all about the same wavy lines and forms.

Actually, hills and mountains have countless shapes and sizes. Observe them with care.

Sketches of fjords in Norway, made from a boat, indicate the variety and intricacy of hill and mountain formations.

Blasted, quarried rocks are sharp-edged; rocks exposed to erosion by water over long periods have rounded edges.

Sketching trees

Trees exist wherever human beings live, except in the Arctic and Antarctic regions. Observe trees honestly, instead of thinking of them in terms of pieces of wood, much wider at the base than higher up, with big branches radiating in every direction from about halfway up. More often than not, a tree painted by a beginner looks like an old-fashioned coat-and-hatrack with a mass of green hay or green cloth piled on its top. Look at trees with care. There are countless species of them and every tree is different.

Sketching foliage

In my youth, I considered myself quite up-to-date by painting trees like huge green bundles standing on dark brown stems. A very famous artist explained that foliage, even in the densest jungle, allows birds, small and big, to fly or hop from branch to branch, through the apparently impenetrable mass of leaves. I learnt a priceless lesson. I now always render the anatomy of the tree, its entire trunk and main branches, before adding the foliage.

Except for the painstakingly trimmed trees, popular in formal gardens, natural foliage is in sections. Each section is discernible by its lights and shadows, besides its outlines. Don't draw each leaf, but do observe the shapes of the main sections and remember that the biggest branches grow out of the trunk, the smaller branches grow out of the big branches, and the twigs out of the small branches. The leaves grow out of the twigs. No part of a tree hangs in mid-air.

Sketching marine subjects

The higher up you are when looking at a body of water, the more you see; the lower you are, the less you see. One of the big problems of beginners is that they always think of the sea or a lake as an immense expanse of water. They paint the end of the water, the horizon, close to the top of the support. When you're standing or sitting on a shore, the end of the water, that is, the line where water and sky meet, is quite low. Exactly as low as your own eye level.

Placing the end of the water high causes it to look as if the water were standing up, like a rippled glass panel of a shower stall. Observe what you really see, instead of using preconceived notions.

Sketching the city

Many beginners paint one house next to the other, all facing the onlooker, every window and door shown in its rectangular shape. In reality, you only see houses in this fashion directly across the street. As you walk up or down the street, or look right or left from your window, you see houses at an angle, and the higher up you are, the more of the city you see. The aim of a fine artist is to paint a picture, not a topographical view or an architectural rendering. He must look for the most attractive views in a city.

Trees, as many beginners think they look.

Trees, bushes, plants are all different; they have to be observed like everything else you want to depict.

These trees were sketched in Buenos Aires. Many of them have trunks which look like monsters.

Can a city be picturesque?

This is a question occasionally asked by people who detest the city and are prejudiced against it. "The city is all right to visit, but I wouldn't live there if they gave it to me." But cities can be, and are beautiful, except perhaps some of the modern housing projects in which every unit is the same. Cities which have evolved in the course of centuries offer much inspiration to artists. Different houses, various colors, awnings, parks, trees, statues, store signs, traffic itself, in sunlight, rain, snow, in the evening, at night, all this becomes a most attractive theme in the hands of an artist.

Pay attention to proportions, main forms, colors, variety of styles. Sketch the biggest sections first, the entire pattern of buildings, before adding details of any sort. Don't start painting or sketching a street scene by depicting one person, with the intention of adding the rest afterwards. Do the whole view, the street, the houses, stores, before adding the figures in general, and perhaps one special figure in particular.

Importance of details

The use of details in any painting depends upon the size of the picture and your style. A magic realist wants every possible detail; an impressionist wants a general effect; the average traditional painter likes to show details of important and nearby objects. There are times when the omission of details causes parts of your picture to seem empty. In a small painting, where the window of a house is ½" high, you can hardly paint details. But if the window is 3" high, you don't want to paint a blue or gray spot without indicating the framework.

It's well worth your while sketching such details with care, on a larger scale.

Shading in sketches

Shading is usually helpful in rendering forms, but don't carry it to the point where your sketch looks like a finished picture. Work in lines, and add shading where it helps you understand the forms.

Color in sketches

Fully realistic coloring in sketches is time-consuming and often literally impossible, due to a lack of time and a lack of the proper colors. All you can expect to do is to add colors in color-pencils, felt brush pens, or by writing the names of colors on your outline sketches. But even the crudest colors do help you to remember the actual colors. For example, a rock may be brownish, grayish, yellowish. A house may be blue, green, pink, ocher, and so forth. A few strokes with the color-pencil closest to the actual shade will act as reminders later on.

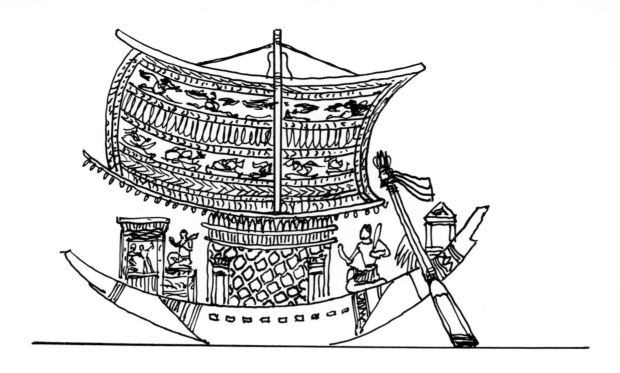

On the top a gentleman's pleasure boat, a beautiful, nicely-detailed drawing from an ancient Egyptian tomb. It shows the boat in a diagrammatic form. In reality, the boat would look like the one on the bottom, seen at an angle.

(Above Left) Street as seen from street level. Horizontal lines seem to be going upward or downward. A car a block away is so small that it could be pushed through one window of the car nearby. (Above Right) Street corner seen from fourth-floor window. Top of small houses is almost horizontal, but lower lines go upward. This is perspective. (Below) Looking down, originally vertical lines in houses on the other side of the avenue converge. Store windows appear to be smaller in height than ordinary windows on the third floor.

5 Linear perspective

PERSPECTIVE SEEMS TO BE the most frightening word, in any language, for art students. It's a kind of boogeyman. "If I only knew perspective!" or "Do you think I can ever learn perspective?" or "Couldn't we be without perspective?" are common questions and exclamations among art students. Yet, there's nothing terrifying about perspective. It's like swimming—once you learn it you'll never forget it.

What is perspective?

The word perspective has three meanings: 1. It's the visual appearance of things, as compared with their diagrammatic shapes. 2. The rendering of three dimensional objects and scenes on a flat, two dimensional surface in such a manner that you create an illusion of three dimensions. 3. We say, figuratively, that we see something in perspective, when we look at personal, political, or historical events from a distance, perhaps long after the events, thus being able to obtain an over-all idea of the event in connection with previous, concurrent and/or consequent happenings.

Perspective and photography

If perspective was difficult to understand in past ages, when artists had to rely on their eyes and minds, it ought to be easy enough to grasp in this age of the camera, especially the camera which takes and develops pictures in a few seconds. Machine-made pictures verify man's conclusions concerning perspective. Yet, strangely enough, people are puzzled by slanting, converging lines done by artists, even though they never question the veracity of perspective in photographs. Let's mention at this point that perspective in humans, animals, and small objects is usually called foreshortening.

Who discovered perspective?

Some twenty-five centuries ago, the Greeks, noted for their logical and philosophical thinking and for their unsurpassed ability to observe, discovered that when a ship appeared on the horizon one could only see the tip of the mast. After a while, the crow's nest, the top of the sail and, gradually, more and more of the ship became visible. The Greeks also noticed that the boat appeared to grow bigger and bigger as it neared port. The Greeks deducted that the earth must be spherical; otherwise, the entire ship would be visible all the time. And they deducted that things appear to be smaller according to distance—the first rule of perspective.

The classic Greeks noticed that ships looked smaller in the distance, and lines drawn through bottoms and tops converged into one point in the back.

Converging lines

Through geometric calculations, the Greeks found that if they drew straight lines across the tip of the mast and the bottom of a ship nearby, and the tip of the mast and the bottom of a similar ship faraway, the two lines would exactly demarcate the tips and the bottoms of similar ships anywhere between these two ships. They also noticed that the bottom line appeared to run upward, the top line seemed to run downward, even though, in reality, the two lines had to be horizontal and parallel. This discovery established the second rule of perspective: the rule of receding, converging lines.

Theory and practice in classic Greece

Most large paintings in antiquity were executed on walls; as walls were destroyed by fire, earthquake, natural deterioration or human neglect, few such paintings have survived. We have descriptions by contemporary travelers and writers, and small-scale imitations of murals on Attic pottery. While draftsmanship on these ceramics is often wonderful and clearly shows foreshortened arms, hands and heads, none of the vase pictures has any background or foreground.

This lack of pictorial background is attributed to what is called *horror vacui,* horror of emptiness, which seems to have afflicted the ancient Greeks. In all likelihood, their large paintings also lacked realistic backgrounds, although some rocks and trees were represented with the figures which always dominated those paintings. But linear perspective, linear changes in diagrammatic forms, were scientifically rendered.

Perspective in classic Rome

A truly remarkable knowledge of perspective developed in ancient Rome. Murals in Pompeii, Herculaneum, the City of Rome and mosaic pictures, especially in the North African colonies of the Roman Empire, give ample proof of a full understanding of perspective among Roman artists. Those pictures also prove that there have always been good, bad, and mediocre artists.

Evolution of perspective

All but forgotten during the Dark Ages, perspective began to be practiced by the end of the thirteenth century and early in the fourteenth, gradually evolving into a perfect science. Painters vied with each other in rendering architectural backgrounds in so realistic a fashion that the onlooker felt he could walk right up the steps, around the columns, and so forth.

By the seventeenth century, they painted architectural units which looked like the real thing. By a curious coincidence, this eye-cheating approach was very fashionable in Europe long before the discovery of Pompeii, with its remarkable murals using similar architectural elements with surprising skill.

Exaggerations in perspective

El Greco (1541–1614) and Michelangelo (1475–1564) exaggerated and distorted figures, motions, gestures, and props, largely, no doubt, on account of temperament. About a hundred years ago, distortions began to play an important role in Western art. Artists claimed to have individual ways of seeing things. But in every case, from El Greco to Picasso, from Michelangelo to Lipchitz, from Tintoretto to Kokoschka, exaggerations and distortions were based on sound knowledge. There's a difference between mistakes due to ignorance, and deliberate exaggerations.

It may not always be easy for a student or a layman to distinguish this difference, just as it may not be easy or even possible for a layman to recognize the difference between the finest ruby and an artificial stone. The point is that you have to know things. A knowledge of perspective is of vital significance in outdoor subjects in which spatial relationship is always involved.

Let's look at basic rules

Most people walk up or down a street without being conscious of perspective. As they walk on, every house, store, sign, door, window becomes full-size when people pass them. I heard a fascinating story about a man born blind who, many years later, gained eyesight through a remarkable operation which could have been performed earlier, had the family known about the possibility of such surgery. The man was intelligent, and had learned as much as a blind person could. With his newly-gained eyesight, he began to check up on his knowledge.

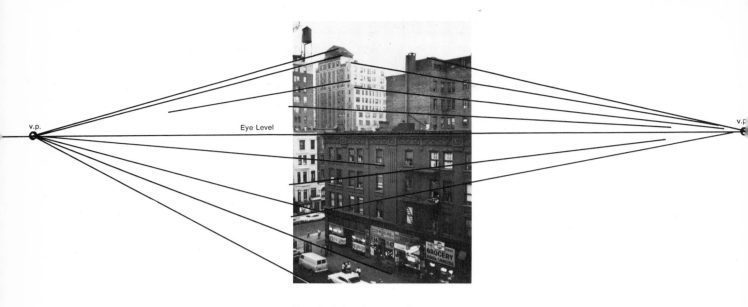

Parallel, horizontal lines below the eye level go up, similar lines above
the eye level go down, all into the same vanishing point (v.p.).

It's the same, no matter where you are.

He had one perplexing, and at first frightening, experience, a visual fact nobody had ever mentioned to him. The experience came as he began to walk outdoors and noticed that cars, trucks, people, dogs, and everything else seemed to be growing bigger and bigger as they came closer to him. He began to run at the sight of oncoming cars because he expected them to blow up.

Views from the window

Looking out the window from the back of the room, you have a small view of whatever is across the street: houses, sky, hills, scenery. If there are houses across the street, you can normally see three or four floors, with two or three windows on each floor through your window, which is about three feet wide and six feet high. In the country, your view encompasses a large part of the scenery.

Move closer to the window

As you move closer to your window, you see more and more, until your nose touches the window pane, when you behold a whole city block of houses or a considerable expanse of the countryside. This is the simplest proof of the fact that all objects diminish according to distance. If an artist told you he can paint a lifesize picture of all the houses in a New York City block, or a large part of the Grand Canyon, on a support no larger than your window, you'd think he was kidding or that he had some trick up his sleeve. Yet what we see through the window is the actual visual size.

Circle of vision

As you move closer to, or step back from the window, you see more or less, according to distance. What you see fits into a circle, your circle of vision. Have you ever tried to concentrate on one view, without moving your head and without batting an eyelash? Whether you are indoors or outdoors, the view you can behold with one direct look is this circle of vision. Actually, though, our eyes are constantly moving, in every direction, so that we see the surroundings, too.

Since our eyes are round, we're bound to see literally in circles. Round pictures would be closer to reality than the oblong pictures we usually produce. At the same time, we are able to see the surroundings, and we know those surroundings are there. The human eye eliminates the hazy or fuzzy appearance outside the circle of vision. In photography, we notice that objects on the left and right sides are slightly curved inward, even though the finer lenses used in a camera are made in such a manner as to compensate for this natural distortion.

What happens to basic forms in perspective?

A square looks like a square only when seen directly from the front-center. The moment you move it, or yourself, in any direction, the square ceases to

|← 42″ →| |← 42″ →|

(Left) You can see a large part of a house through a window much smaller than what you see through it, when you're twelve feet from the window in the room. (Right) At a distance of seven feet from your window, you see much more. You can paint half a block of a New York City street on a support 42″ wide and 38″ high, in the actual size in which you see that half block.

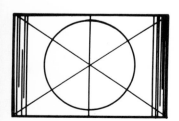
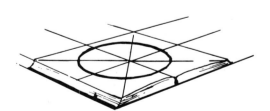
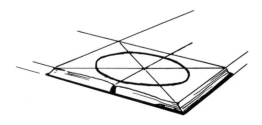

Place a round plate on an open book and observe the shapes of book and plate from various angles: right or left, higher or lower. The shapes are different from every viewpoint.

be rectangular visually. A circle looks like a circle from the front. From any other angle, it acquires the visual shape of an ellipse, leaning in various directions, narrower or wider, according to the angle from which you're looking at it. All other shapes, geometric or free, go through similar changes. There's only one object in the whole world which never changes its shape: the sphere. The reason is obvious. The sphere is three dimensionally the same from every possible viewpoint.

Place a round plate on a rectangular book and look at the combination from different angles: lower your head, move it higher, one way or another, and the two simple objects will look different. There's a very old method of proving these changes: cut a square piece of cardboard, draw a circle on it so that the circle should touch the center of each of the four sides; draw lines across the center of the circle horizontally, straight up and diagonally, into the corners of the square. Move or tilt this piece of cardboard into a hundred different positions; square, circle, and the lines will form a hundred different patterns.

Three books and a pear

Put a closed book across an open book on the table; place a pear near one corner of the closed book; stand a third book on its narrow bottom behind the two books which are flat on the table. Draw this combination from several angles, merely to see the relationship between the forms; how they change from every angle, even though you never touch the items. The pear, a fairly symmetrical object, won't change very much, but the books change, visually, to such an extent that they will no longer resemble their diagrammatic shapes.

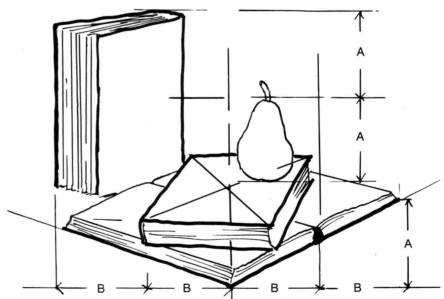

Three books and a pear: a closed book with a pear in one corner, placed on an open book, with a third book standing on one of its narrow ends. Observe the relationship, with the help of guidelines, and by measuring the visual proportions of the various items. Draw the same combination from three or four angles, as you really see them, not as you remember them.

How to observe visual appearance

Forget the basic appearance of articles included in your painting. Learn to see in flat pictures, rather than in three dimensional space. You work on a flat surface; you have to reduce everything to two dimensions. All objects and all combinations of objects form designs or patterns. Depict the pattern as you see it, and all you need for this is honest observation. Each feature of every item must be related to other features. Looking at the three books, for instance, you'll notice that one corner of a book is near a corner of another book, with a certain space between the two. This space happens to have a triangular shape. Observe the triangular shape as if it were a real object, and draw the space in this shape. It's always possible to find such simple shapes in any subject.

Negative shapes help

Spaces between objects are called negative shapes, as against the positive shapes of the objects themselves. You'll always find such negative shapes and they are bound to help you in establishing the positive shapes. There's a closed book on top of an open book. What shapes do you see on the open book, not covered by the closed book? How much of the standing book is blocked out by the two other books? How high is the pear or the stem of the pear compared with the standing book? If you connect two corners with a straight line, how does that straight line slant: right or left? How much right or how far left?

The importance of guidelines

Lines drawn, actually or in your imagination, across certain points in your picture are called guidelines. We use guidelines in every walk of life . . . why not in drawing and painting? Such lines show you the relationship between forms, visually. You might, of course, use your view finder, if you've made one. You can easily find true perspective and proportions when looking through the grid of a view finder.

What about articles behind each other?

I've known art students who drew and painted objects one next to the other, although those items were set up on a table, one in front, another one behind, and so forth. The pictures looked as if they represented a shelf in a store, with various items displayed on it, one next to the other. Visually—that is, in perspective—articles in the back seem to be higher than those in the front. How much higher? This depends upon the sizes of the objects and the space between them. Study this at home by simply arranging a few articles on a table, one behind the other, and looking at them from a higher and a lower viewpoint. The higher you are, the more space you see between the objects, and this means that, visually, the base of an object in the rear is that much higher than the base of an object in the front. Observe the visual distance, and draw it that way.

Perspective outdoors

Whether you look at books, pears, and other small articles, or at houses, trees and roads, you'll see a pattern formed by the combination of items. A very big tree in the background has to look bigger than a very small tree in the foreground, even though distance causes it to appear smaller in height and width. You have to measure, visually, one thing against another. Where does the base of the distant tree appear to be compared with the base of a tree nearby? How tall is a tree when measured against a four-story house behind it? How many times does the visual width of a rock formation fit into the width of a door in the house? At what point does the road or path appear to cut across the trunk of a tree? Draw and paint it the way it appears, and the result will be in correct perspective. Draw guidelines across the main forms, horizontally and vertically.

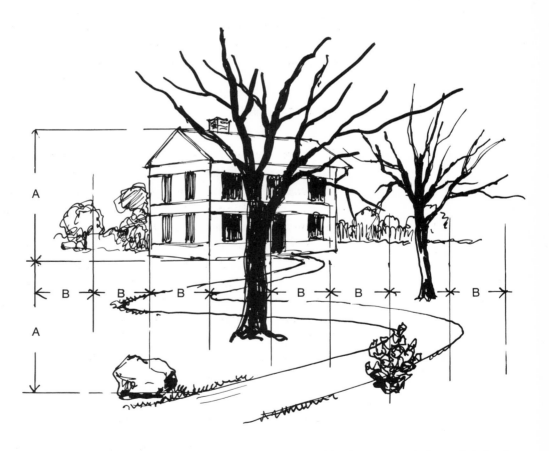

Outdoors, too, shapes, sizes change with distance and viewpoint. Look at the visual pattern: how much of a house is covered by the tree in front? At what points does the winding path cut across the tree, visually? Compare proportions and sizes with the help of guidelines. How far is one item from another, visually, not in reality?

Horizon or eye level

Whatever is below the horizon seems to be running upward; whatever is above the horizon appears to run downward. Thus, sidewalks, curbs, railroad tracks, roads, rivers go up; eaves, rooftops, telegraph wires go down. What is the horizon? To most people, the horizon is as far as the eye can see, on the ocean, where the water meets the sky. Anything beyond the horizon is invisible. But a horizon exists everywhere, not only on the ocean, where nature practically draws the horizon clear across the picture.

There's a horizon in mountains, in the jungle, in the city. It isn't a positively fixed line; it moves wherever you go, because it's your own eye level. If you sit on the beach, your eye level is only about 25″ or 30″ above the ground. If you stand up, your eye level grows up to the level of your eyes; if you climb to the top of a mountain, your eye level doggedly goes with you.

We see more from a higher level

The higher up we are, the more we see. Even on a ship, you see more from the crow's nest than from the deck; that's why the crow's nest was invented and that's why observation towers used to be erected in very ancient times: one can see farther from the top and notice the activities of an approaching enemy. Now, we can go higher than ever, by flying. Looking down from a plane, we literally have a bird's-eye view of the world, a view very different from the way we behold things standing, sitting, or walking on this earth.

Vanishing points

As I said before, all lines below the horizon run upward, while lines above the horizon run downward. Let's add that all parallel, horizontal lines run into one point on the horizon: into the so-called vanishing point. Every horizontal line on one wall of even the tallest building runs into one-and-the-same vanishing point. On another wall of the same building, all parallel horizontal lines run into another vanishing point. There are as many vanishing points as there are different groups of horizontal parallel lines, but all these vanishing points are on the same eye level or horizon.

Vanishing points are not decided arbitrarily. Draw the top-most line of a structure downwards and the bottom-most line of the same structure upwards: they meet in one point—which is the vanishing point—and, at the same time, it's the eye level. If you look at a building from an angle, the vanishing point on one side will be much farther from the building than it will on the other side.

How to determine directions of lines

Horizontal and vertical lines ought to be easy enough to determine. We normally walk or stand on a horizontal floor; regular buildings have vertical walls, vertical columns; lampposts are vertical or, as the general public calls it: straight up-and-down. The problem is to see the slanting lines—at what angle do they slant, visually? A well-trained eye can tell

The eye level or horizon moves with you. If you sit, your eye level is lower than when you stand or climb to the top of a hill.

As you go higher, the scenery goes lower, visually, whether you look at the sea or at a city.

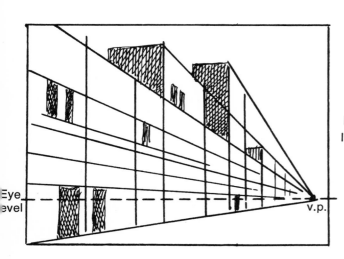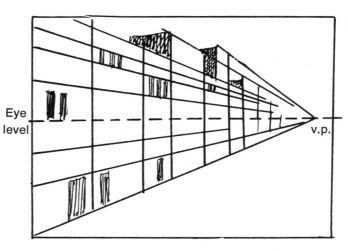

Geometric construction of street view from lower and higher levels.

whether it's a 30°, a 45°, or a 60° angle, but I must warn you not to trust your eye until you're sure it has been trained. There are too many optical illusions around us. Things are not what they seem to be. This is true in art as well as in politics and other fields.

Visual measuring of directions

There's a well-established method of measuring directions in art visually, employed by the old masters and modern masters as well. Hold a full-length pencil with your thumb and index finger in such a manner that the pencil is at a right angle to your thumb. Let your other fingers support the pencil. Keep your hand about 15″ from one of your eyes and close the other eye. Move your whole hand at the wrist without changing the relationship between your fingers and the pencil. The hand and the pencil must remain parallel with your forehead, as if it were moving in one plane.

Turn your wrist until the pencil is aligned with the main direction of a form, the roof of a house, for example. You can also look at a winding or curved line this way, to find the main direction of the curve. Pull your pencil and hand down directly onto your support, and you'll see the correct angle of any line. You may have to repeat this a couple of times before you understand the simplicity of the method.

The importance of proportions

Proportions are more important than most people, including artists, seem to realize. Proportions refer to the comparative sizes of all parts of an object, and to comparative sizes of all objects in the same picture. The ancient Greeks established what they considered perfect proportions in human figures and in architecture. There was no deviation from those ideals in Greek art. Although we admire these Greek proportions, we needn't accept them as perfect, because perfection is a debatable quality; standards of beauty vary according to civilizations and periods.

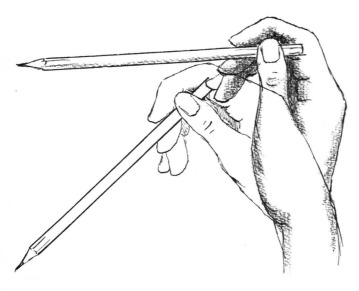

Visual measuring of directions: hold a pencil or any straight stick as shown in the illustration, so that your thumb is at a right angle (90 degrees) to the stick. Don't stretch your arm in this measuring; hold it about 15″ from your face. Turn your wrist until the stick covers the visual, not the actual three dimensional, direction of the object. This object may be the roof of a building, a street curb, the general direction of a curving road or river. What you see with the stick is the direction of a line or form in perspective. In other words, the direction reduced to a two dimensional picture.

Are correct proportions necessary? Yes, in realistic work. No, in abstraction. As long as you're interested in realistic renderings, you have to observe proportions. Let me give you a couple of unforgettable examples. Some years ago, an acquaintance of mine, a dilettante who thought he was a great, but unrecognized artist, showed me a painting of Venice he had done in oils. There were houses with very high Gothic windows on a shore, fir trees in front of the houses on the left. The firs looked like artificial Christmas trees. On the right, there were three or four gondolas—one in full, the others partly visible, all with the well-known ornaments on their long-necked prows.

The painter had never been in Venice, but had heard about it. He didn't even consider it necessary to borrow some picture postcards showing the famous city. He believed that houses were built there on small, but real islands, with a little beach and trees in front of each house. He had no idea that the fronts of houses in Venice emerge directly from the water and that vegetation is possible only in small rear courtyards, not on the side of the canal.

Such mistakes are characteristic of artists painting realistic scenes from imagination. The worst feature of the picture was that the windows were incredibly big: the fir trees might have been small potted plants on a windowsill. And the gondolas, which in reality are quite long, were so small in this painting that they could have flown in and out every window, including the gondoliere and his long oar, with the greatest of ease.

More recently, I visited the one-man show of an artist who painted mostly snowscapes, New England houses with front porches, and people in colorful skating or skiing garbs tobogganing or frolicking in front of each house. The style was bold, impressionistic. The artist, a very modest young woman, asked me to tell her my frank opinion. I did. I told her that all the figures were too big in proportions. "How could that be?" she asked. "Aren't the figures smaller and smaller according to distance?" They were, but not correctly so. Each figure or group of figures was too big for the house in front of which it happened to be. Indicating horizontal lines from the entrance of each house to the feet and heads of the respective figures, I showed her that the humans were much taller than the doors through which they would have to enter and leave their houses.

The young woman burst out in laughter at her own childish mistake and thanked me for my criticism. She later made the doors and houses bigger. It would have been too difficult to make the figures smaller. Such instances prove again and again that knowledge, intelligence and good judgment are as important as natural talent.

Visual measuring of proportions

The simplest method for measuring proportions is to look at everything through your grid-lined view finder. Another well-established method, employed by every realistic artist I ever heard of, is to hold a pencil, a straight stick or even a small ruler, pressing it with your thumb against your index and middle finger in such a manner that the pencil or stick stands straight up-and-down. The bottom of the stick can be kept fast by holding it between

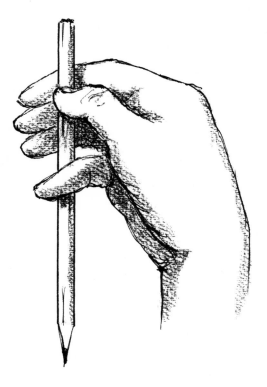

Visual measuring of proportions: stretch your arm fully while holding a pencil or any straight stick in such a manner that you can move your thumb up and down, without changing the position of the stick. The tip of your stick represents the top of whatever you're measuring; your thumb slides up or down until it's exactly at the bottom of the item. This length of the stick between the tip and your thumb is the visual size of the object. Move your hand and stick up and down, right or left, counting how many times that basic size is in the total width or height. For example, how much wider is a house than a rock formation? How long is an automobile compared with the height of the house behind it?

your fourth finger and your little finger. Stretch your arm as far as it goes; close one eye; hold the stick so that its tip is even with the top of whatever you're measuring. Move your thumbnail down until it's even with the bottom of the section you're measuring. You now have a length between your thumb and the tip of the stick, representing the visual, not the actual, size of the object. Without moving your head or shoulders, keeping the stick at the same distance from your eye, move it down, as many times as needed to cover the rest of the object or scenery. You can measure the width of something in the same fashion, by holding your stick horizontally or at a slant.

My advice is that you first try to draw proportions from direct observation. Once they're on the support, however, use the method described above and check up on your eye judgment. The chances are that you'll be astonished to see how many mistakes your unaided eye had made.

Perspective and shadows

Although strictly linear perspective can be absolutely correct, shading helps you in seeing forms. It's a good idea to indicate at least the main shadows, even in a quick line sketch. Observe the visual appearance of shadows, their sizes and proportions, with as much care as you observe the lines.

6 Color perspective

IT WAS ONLY LONG AFTER THE REDISCOVERY and development of linear perspective that artists of Western Europe noticed and began to render another kind of perspective: perspective in color. They realized that objects do not merely diminish in size as they move farther and farther away, but they also become bluish in color. Color perspective refers to changes in hues and shades due to distance and atmospheric conditions.

Blue distance

At first, only a small section—the center of the most distant part of the scenery in a painting—was done in shades of blue. Later, the entire background was painted in subdued tones, but it wasn't until the early nineteenth century that John Constable and Joseph Mallord William Turner discovered true color perspective.

Impressionism

The Impressionist school, the first of our "modern" trends in art, was based on strictly on-the-spot observation. The artist's aim was to depict what he saw at a glance, emphasizing color, motion, and atmospheric conditions, rather than delineating buildings, trees, carriages, humans and animals in every detail, according to long-established academic formulas.

Aerial perspective?

Artists began to speak of aerial perspective. They meant the changes wrought by the amount of air between the painter and his subject, and the changes due to the condition of the air: sunny, foggy, snowy, rainy, and so forth. The term "aerial perspective" was valid until man began to fly. Looking down from a plane, linear perspective is quite different from what we see walking on solid earth. Tall buildings look smaller at the bottom than at the top because the bottom is farther away. Vertical lines, the walls of buildings, lampposts, and the like, converge when viewed from the air. Aerial perspective now refers to photographs or paintings made from flying machines. What we used to call aerial perspective is now color perspective, because it probes the changes in color, due to whatever reason.

Main features of color perspective

Colors become lighter, hazier at about the same ratio as lines recede and objects diminish in visual size, but the weather must also be considered.

On a cloudy, rainy day, colors are entirely different from those on a sunny day, and you cannot see as far as on a bright day. Hills and clouds often blend into each other on a cloudy day. Against a brilliant sky at sunset, distant hills seem very much darker than sections of the scenery nearby.

Watch out for bright hues

One of the most common mistakes made by beginners is to paint very bright-hued objects—such as an orange sweater, a yellow tent, a brilliant red skirt—as the respective colors squeezed from the tubes, no matter how far in the distance those items may be. You have to compare those colors with the same hues nearby and you'll see they are much lighter, hazier in the background. There are different shades in yellow, orange, and red as well as in all other colors.

What is color value?

White is the lightest, black is the darkest color the human eye can perceive. All other colors are between these two extremes. The value of any color depends upon how close it is to white or to black. Compare every color, every shade, with one or the other, or with both of these two extreme colors. If you paint any hue darker than it ought to be, according to distance and weather conditions, that hue will seem to be a hole in the picture. Paint something too light, and it will appear to jump out of the picture or look like something accidentally stuck onto it.

It's a simple and practical idea to place a piece of pure white material, perhaps just a paper tissue, on the ground, or hang it on a tree, so that you might compare all colors with that piece of white. Color is meaningless in art without establishing the right shade of it. Even abstract and non-objectve painters often want to achieve effects of depth. If so, they have to bear in mind the importance of values.

Local color and visual color

With the exception of certain theoretically colorless substances, such as pure water and colorless glass, everything has a color, made by nature or by man. This is what we call *local color*. We speak of a blue carpet, a red shirt, green grass. The *visual color* is not the same, though. There are highlights and shadows; different sources of light: sun, candle, gas, white or pink neon, firelight, and so on. Every type of illumination affects the local colors of objects. You wouldn't buy a suit or a dress without looking at it by daylight. Or would you?

Forget the names of colors

When painting, forget the names of colors. Observe every shade, every value. Paint what you actually see, by comparing one hue with its surroundings. Grass is green, but it may be brownish, yellowish, bluish, light, dark, in scores of shades.

(Left) Consider values: if you paint everything equally dark or strong, you'll have a flat design, instead of a realistic painting. (Center) Clouds and distant mountains are just a couple of shades darker than the sky. Sections nearer are more detailed and brighter in hue. (Right) Clouds aren't torn pieces of paper. They're soft, fluffy, roundish. The sky is darker on top than at the bottom, whether it's bright blue or rainy, cloudy.

The sea may be slightly rippled or wavy, with whitecaps. It has many colors and values. If you paint it all one color it'll resemble a rippled glass wall in a shower stall.

Distant hills and mountains

In a landscape of mountainous scenery, your whole painting often depends upon such a background for interest, beauty, and artistry. Yet most students paint distant mountains too big and too strong in colors, even if they paint them bluish in tone. Women have a clever way of describing colors as two shades lighter, one shade darker, one shade more green in it, and so on. These may not be professional descriptions, but they work. Two shades represents a slightly bigger difference than one shade. And that's enough to make a pocketbook or a belt just right. It can do the same to a mountain in your painting.

What about the sea?

The sea isn't blue. Not even the Mediterranean is blue. It has a variety of colors, ranging from light, bright green or blue to violet, dark blue, dark green and even purple. Usually, the water is darker than the sky by daylight, but the difference may be one shade. Occasionally, there's a stripe of darker tone across the water, or halfway across, but that, too, should be carefully observed for value. The water reflects the atmosphere. It's darker, more grayish on a stormy, cloudy day; it's lighter, more bluish on a bright, sunny day. The moon or the sun is reflected in water. If the water is calm, the reflection is well defined. On rough water, only the tops of waves reflect the colors in a sparkling fashion.

The colors of the sea change continually. Every ten or fifteen minutes, there's a considerable difference. You have to establish the colors quickly, but there's no reason why you shouldn't change some of them if you like another color better. Generally speaking, a seascape is easier to paint correctly when the shore is included. You can compare shacks, rocks, beach, perhaps figures, with each other.

Color perspective in cityscapes

Even if you paint a straight row of houses across the street, indicate the fact that those houses are not touching the tip of your nose. Make them less bright, less detailed. If you depict a street going away from you, compare buildings of the same color at different distances. For example, look at a gray house a block away, and one right next to you. Make sure that the building in the distance is in a lighter, hazier tone than that of a building of the same hue in the foreground.

Shadows are as much darker than the illuminated sections in the distance as they are in the foreground. That is, both shadow and illuminated part are stronger in the foreground than in the rear. Once you know these facts you'll see them without any effort and substitute real observation for preconceived notions.

7 Lights, shadows, atmospheric moods

IN YOUR STUDIO, you can easily provide the right light for painting. You either have daylight or artificial illumination; you always have the light coming from the left if you're right-handed, coming from the right if you happen to be left-handed. The shadows are always the same, on the opposite side of the light. Outdoors, you face the problem of continuously changing light and shadow because of the sun's changing position in the sky.

There are two kinds of shadows

There can be no light without shadow. *Local shadows* are the shadows you see on the sides of an object not directly illuminated by the source of light. The light also throws the shadow of every object on the ground, on the wall behind the object, or onto neighboring objects. This is called the *cast shadow*.

Shadows move with the source of light

Artificial light is normally fixed; the sun, however, climbs higher and the cast shadows become shorter, while the local shadows change in form. At noontime, there's only a small shadow at the base of an object, while its top is completely lighted. In the afternoon, as the sun moves downward, in the opposite direction, the cast shadows grow longer and longer, also in the opposite direction, while the local shadows are completely reversed from their morning appearance.

In midsummer, when the days are long, you can work for a few hours at a stretch without noticeable change in the shadows. As the days become shorter, the difference is more evident.

I used to know an artist who started to paint a group of ornate, Baroque houses in Italy. Each house had rich, high relief ornaments around windows and doors. The artist was strictly traditional, trying to paint every detail. He made a good pencil drawing before applying watercolors, without, however, indicating the shadows. Instead of establishing an over-all effect in color, he did one house after the other. After the first house on the left, he began to paint the second house, the third, the fourth, finishing the last house on the right by late afternoon. Totally involved in realism as he was, he painted the shadows on and next to the ornaments as they looked when he was working on each particular section. As a result, they were all in different directions. The first ones on the right, the middle ones straight below, the last ones on the left; the shadows done at midday were much longer downward than the others, because the sun was high above the houses at the time. Each house represented a different time of the day.

As the light moves, so do the shadows. Watch out for these changes when working outdoors. On long summer days, the changes are slower, not so conspicuous. On shorter days, the light-and-shadow effects change very quickly.

Local and cast shadows depend upon the position of the source of light. The higher the light, the shorter the shadow. The shape of a cast shadow is a combination of the shape of the object and the shape of the surface on which the shadow is cast. Shadows are also seen in perspective. Thus, the cast shadow of a disc looks like an ellipse.

If you want to finish such a painting in one day, lay out all lights and shadows at the same time, and stick to this layout, regardless of the changes in the light-and-shadow effect. One of the basic principles in painting is to work all over the support, rather than to finish one section before going to the next. Indoors, where the light doesn't change, the section-by-section painting might come out all right. Outdoors, you can make disturbing errors.

Shapes and sizes of shadows

Local shadows follow the forms of the articles themselves: they are roundish on an apple, straight and sharp on a house. Cast shadows assume the combined shapes of the objects and of the surfaces upon which they're cast. Thus, shadows can be wavy, they can climb up a wall or curtain, go downstairs or upstairs. The length of the shadow is controlled by the object and by the position of the source of light. The lower the light, the longer the shadow. When you walk early in the morning, with the rising sun behind you, you have a gigantically long shadow in front of you.

Shadows have sizes, shapes, perspective, color, and value, like any actual object. It's a grave and common mistake just to add a little smudge at the base and to one side of an object, and to call the smudge a shadow. Colors of shadows vary according to the colors of the objects involved and according to the light. Although shadows usually seem to be dark, they are not necessarily black or even very dark. Look at them with care; compare them with the darkest colors in the picture and with each other. Shadows on snow can never be as dark as shadows on grass. The deepest shadow on a whitewashed building is only a few shades darker than white: a very light gray, often bluish in tone.

Hide-and-seek sun

On a cloudy and windy day, the sun sometimes seems to be playing hide-and-seek. This natural phenomenon is somewhat hard on the eyes and makes painting difficult as the constant change of lights and shadows interferes with the observation of colors and values. It makes an interesting picture, though, when shadows glide across hills, valleys, trees, houses, mountains as fast as the wind blows.

Depicting such a scene demands careful watching of the general effect, rather than trying to determine the shape of every shadow dashing uphill and downhill. Observe how dark the shadows are against the bright colors, and what variation there is among them. Your best bet is to first paint the scenery without indicating shadows. Then go over the scene, here and there, with a glaze of the color and value of the shadow. Use oil glazes in oil painting, transparent washes in all water media.

Is prettiness important?

Many people think a painting must be pretty, cheerful. Mayor Fiorello H. La Guardia was one of those people. At the opening of a big exhibition at

Cast shadows are broken when they hit a wall, curtain, steps or some other obstacle. They literally seem to be walking upstairs or downstairs.

The Metropolitan Museum of Art, he flatly declared, in his high-pitched voice: "I don't care what anyone says, art is art only if it's pretty." He added immediately that "I've been told by my friends who are here with me, before we came up here, not to talk about something I know nothing about, and to keep my big, fat mouth shut." And, naturally, he was greeted with loud laughter for his candor.

The fact is that prettiness is not judged by any universal standard, and if prettiness even in the Western sense were the criterion, what would we do with the *Sistine Chapel Ceiling* by Michelangelo, with El Greco's *Burial of Count Orgaz,* or with any of the innumerable paintings representing the Crucifixion?

Atmospheric moods

The morning sun is a cool yellow, and every object illuminated by it reflects that tone. In the afternoon, the sun turns warmer in color, more and more reddish. By sunset, the sun is a big orange dangling above the earth. All walls, trees, roads, human and animal figures and other objects reflect this color, and the shadows change with the light. There's no definite color scheme one can learn from a book. The only method is to observe everything honestly. Use your own eyes, but remember to compare one red, one green, one blue, one yellow, and so forth, with another shade of the same color. Subtlety, a slight underplaying, is much better than exaggeration.

Work on a painting several times

A sunset is always unique. You'll never see the same one again. It's like a kaleidoscope: the ingredients are the same but color and design combinations vary to eternity. Other moods, however, are repeated almost every

Hide-and-seek sun: on a sunny day with many, but not very big, clouds, a good breeze chases the clouds across the sky, and the shadows of the clouds dash across valleys, hills, houses, trees, mountains, just as fast. Paint the scenery first, then add the shadows, perhaps by glazing or by applying washes over the scenery, indicating the shape of the terrain or object with the curvature of the cast shadow in each section.

day. You might work on an early morning or dusk subject several times, provided that you paint only when the colors and mood are the same.

Make a good layout first, so that you have no problem in finding shapes and sizes, and might concentrate on colors alone. Watch out for contrasts, especially. The difference between darks and lights at dusk is not nearly as strong as by sunlight. The colors of shadows vary according to the local colors and the time of day. There are as many colors in shadows as in light parts.

Clouds

Clouds, light or dark, rain clouds or storm clouds alike, have to be observed for a while. Watch them swirl and continuously change their shapes, billowing, fusing with other clouds, moving in one direction or another. Follow these motions with your brush and, naturally, with the proper colors. Here, too, avoid exaggerations. The darkest cloud is unlikely to be jet black, and the whitest cloud is seldom really white. It's interesting to watch some light seep through the clouds or break through here and there, when the sun is up behind or above the clouds. Clouds are soft . . . an aeroplane can fly through what looks like a very dense cloud. Paint them soft, don't make them appear to be torn pieces of rags hanging in midair. A cloudy sky gives everything a sort of grayish tone, like a veil.

Storm at sea

Spend a little time watching the movement of waves, the pounding of the sea on rocks, the swift streaks or spots of light sparkling on small waves. There's nothing haphazard about all this. Everything has a rhythm and you can paint that after thorough observation. A sea can be stormy under a bright blue sky. In any event, water is liquid, not a hard mass. You have to show it that way by observing its many colors, its motions.

Evening in town

Big cities as well as small towns are enveloped by a gray-blue tone in the evening. The main forms are still clearly visible, but not the small details. Lights appear everywhere, like fireflies. Notice the contrasts, the halos around lights. Test diverse color combinations to find the right one for the desired effect. Orange looks brighter when surrounded by blue and purple; yellow is brighter against light blue; pale green glows against a violet background. There's nothing pitch black on earth. The darkest color is perhaps a reddish blue or a purplish green. Never just plain black.

Snowscapes

Years ago, I painted Washington Square, New York City, from my big studio window on the Square, during a snowfall. Everything looked hazy. The sky was completely gray, the snow was far from white in that light, and had dark streaks left by cars and pedestrians. I thought it was a good impressionist picture and hung it, framed, on a wall. Almost all visitors asked me what the picture represented. I was puzzled as the work was quite realistic, but answered the question with the remark that it was Washington Square, from my window.

The visitors said they didn't see a thing. If it was the Square, where were the windows, the houses, the trees? I suggested that they look closer. "Don't you see the houses and windows, and the barren trees?" "O, so that's what those things are! But why didn't you paint them so one can see them?" I explained that it was a snowy day, when everything is hazy. "What do you mean, hazy? One can see on a snowy day, just as any day." "Not when the snow is falling hard," said I. Then came the most shattering statement: "You say this painting was done while it was snowing? Then where are the snowflakes?" I couldn't ever convince those people that snowflakes are too small to reduce to the size they'd be on a painting 20″ x 30″. Some visitors kept silent, others told me, in no uncertain terms, that snowflakes are snowflakes. Anyone can see them.

Needless to say, people who argued with me were typical laymen. Unfortunately, artists work for laymen, who surely won't buy what they don't like. It's more unfortunate, though, that some art students, and dilettanti, have the same ideas laymen have. Thus, I've seen snowscapes in which the sky was bright blue, while snowflakes were coming down like confetti, splattered with a toothbrush over the finished painting.

Blue sky and snow

This combination of a blue sky with snow is beautiful and possible. The clouds disappear after the snowfall and you have a bright, exhilarating day, with a painting to match, if you paint such a subject. This, by the way, is one of the most salable subjects in the field of outdoor painting. Everybody seems to like white snow, with blue or violet shadows, under a spotless blue sky. If you paint such a subject, pay much attention to the shadows on the snow, as compared with shadows on streets, houses, and so forth. The darkest shadow on the white snow is far from dark. It's only a few shades darker than the snow itself, and shadows in the foreground are darker than those in the distance.

Snow isn't always white

Besides the dirt on snow in cities, snow is not necessarily white even in the country. Sunlight, for instance, is reflected by fresh snow in a very slightly yellowish tone. Towards evening, by the light of the setting sun, an orange tint appears to cover the snow and everything else in the scenery. Try to paint such tones with great gentleness, by merely suggesting them. Don't paint the snow orange or yellow! And although a bright snowy day is most enjoyable, don't forget to wear warm underwear if you work outdoors for any length of time.

Rain or snow, clouds or sunlight, morning, afternoon or evening, spring, summer, autumn or winter, let observation be your guiding spirit in outdoor painting.

8 Reflections in water and shiny objects

IN ONE OF THE MOST FANTASTIC LETTERS I've ever received, a woman described what troubles she'd had trying to depict houses on the shore of a lake. She had painted the houses and trees on the shore in regular oil colors; then painted the water, adding a great deal of varnish to the paint. As soon as the paint was dry to the touch, she flooded the water with more varnish, so that it was as shiny as glass. Yet, to her amazement, the water failed to reflect the houses and trees on the shore. What was she to do?

I patiently explained to her that even a mirror would have to be placed in a horizontal position in order to reflect the image of something standing above it. A mirror at the lower part of the painting, in the same plane as the support, could never possibly reflect the painted section above it; and, surely, even the glossiest oil paints aren't as reflective as a mirror.

Another person asked me, also by mail, how she could make the steps leading up to the porch of a house in her painting look *real shiny?* The steps of her house were newly varnished and she wanted them to look that way in the painting. She'd varnished the steps, leaving the rest of the picture dull, but, somehow or other, the varnished steps didn't reflect the blue sky and the columns of the porch in the painting.

I explained to her that the reflections of the sky and the columns should be painted into the picture, like everything else. Glossy sections of a painting would never reflect what's above those sections in the picture. They'd only reflect things in front of them. A painting is a sort of make-believe. It's an image, not an actual three dimensional thing.

You might say these are extreme cases and I'd agree with you. Still, there must be other people writing similar letters to other artists. Furthermore, countless students have asked me, in person, how to paint shiny objects or reflections in water, pools, puddles or mirrors. This chapter is an answer to all those questions.

Paint all effects as you see them

Calm water reflects everything above it upside down. The tip of a tower or of a tree is at the bottom of the image. A mirror reverses in the same manner if it's below the objects, in a horizontal position. If the mirror is slanted downward, the reflected image in it is slanted backward, and vice-versa. If a mirror is straight in front of something, all objects are reflected in reverse order: what's on the left in reality is on the right in the mirror image. This isn't as commonly known as one might think. I've often been asked by people who saw my self-portraits if I was left-handed, because I was holding a brush in my left hand, in such paintings. That left hand, of course, is my right hand, in real life.

Reflections have to be painted like everything else. Don't expect to varnish the painted water in the lower half of your picture, with the idea that the glossy water will reflect the upper half of the picture. Observe the reflections and paint them as they look. Although the reflected image in the water is directly below the real object on the shore, the reflected image is in perspective, not merely a reversed picture of the original.

Even in a real mirror, the painting is reflected only if the mirror is at a right angle to the picture above. Such a reflection will be flat, and the direct reverse of the original, without any perspective, because the mirror reflects a flat painting, not a real, three dimensional scenery.

Paint the reflections as they are at the time you're watching them. They're often cut across by a rippled path left by a breeze.

Village on the Rhine, with good reflections cut into streaks by rippled water.

Water has ripples

Reflections even in the calmest water are usually cut up by ripples, at least near the bottom, as if broken fragments were floating or jumping towards the shore. There's always a vibration in a body of water and this is clearly seen in the edges of the reflected image. On a lake or sea, a sudden breeze often dashes across the water, leaving a path of ripples, while the rest of the water remains very calm.

Perspective in reflections

There's as much perspective in reflected images as in the actual objects. Distant sections are smaller, and all images are determined by the eye level. Draw this eye level across the picture of a reflecting body of water. The tip of an object in the reflection is as far below the eye level as the actual tip is above the eye level, and the two diminish with distance at an equal rate. If you lie down on the shore, close to the water, you see a larger part of the reflected image than when you stand up or go to a higher ground.

Colors in reflections

No matter how magnificent a reflection may be, perhaps in an artificial reflecting pool, the colors are slightly different from the actual ones. Normally, they're a little hazier, brownish, greenish, or bluish, depending upon the general color of the water. Water may be colorless when poured into a colorless glass, but, as a body, it always has a color.

Pools and puddles

Swimming pools are very common nowadays, and they often make picturesque spots because, as a rule, they are built in odd, not rectangular, shapes, and because most of them are lined with light blue or green tiles. Otherwise, such small artificial pools have little or no pictorial interest, unless you also depict figures in bathing suits with or in the pool. Puddles left by rain in city streets and in the countryside, can be most attractive, though, as they give an unexpected splash of light: reflections in them.

Reflections in puddles are usually fragments of what's above them in reality: perhaps part of a house with a window or door, part of a tree or a passerby. Study such reflections with care and make sure the puddle is of the right size and in the right position, in order to make the reflected images correct. A puddle at a certain distance below a building reflects a certain part of that building. It couldn't reflect any other part in the same position.

Reflections in windows

Remember that windows are not dark holes in, or patches of paint on, walls. They have depth, and they change shape, visually, according to the angle from which you see them. Windows can be open or closed; they may have

Vague reflection in Lake Como. Don't paint from memory, but from direct observation.

Even in what we call mirror-clear water, there are usually thin lines across the picture. Houses or other objects close to the shore are fully seen in the reflected image, but items farther back—as, for example, the steeple in this picture of a Dutch town—may almost completely disappear in perspective.

Reflections in puddles: you see in puddles whatever is directly above them, and as much as has space in the puddle. Here, too, reflected images are in perspective.

Closed windows look dark, except for shades or curtains close to the window panes. The glass usually catches the outside light, especially on the upper floors.

shutters, shades adding a bright color to an otherwise plain wall. Many have lace or textile curtains. The question is: how much of this should you show in your painting? The answer is: no more than you really see from where you're looking at the window.

A friend of mine, sitting in his parked car, once tooted his horn feverishly, trying to attract my attention. Finally, he opened the door and shouted my name. "What's the matter?" he said. "Don't you want to recognize an old friend?" When I told him I couldn't see who was in the car through the windshield, as it was dark inside, he was flabbergasted. "Dark in here? It's as light as outside. I can see you; how come you can't see me?" The fact is that you can look out a window and see everything, provided there's enough light, but you cannot look into a window, unless there's light inside, or unless you push your nose against the glass and shield your eyes with your hands.

Windows catch outside light

Dark, closed windows catch the light or the reflection of the sky, blue or gray, especially on upper floors; they also reflect images of buildings across the street. This is one of the most sensational features of modern steel-and-glass structures, in which entire buildings are reflected, somewhat cut up by the steel frames and distorted by imperfections in the glass panes. These reflections are occasionally enhanced by the fact that some modern buildings employ green or amber glass for protection against sun glare. In the case of the Seagram Building, on New York's Park Avenue, one suspects that the amber color of all outside glass was planned to suggest the product of the company, whiskey. Whatever the reason, such coloring adds interest to a picture, and has to be observed with due care.

Sunlight in windows

Sunlight hitting windows is reflected in an almost blinding glow, especially at sunrise and sunset. Paints do not glow—fine artists don't employ phosphorescent paints, which quickly lose their glow, anyway—so that artists have to observe the contrast between the reflection and the rest of the building. The painting of such effects demands much observation and experimentation as well. Try various combinations in order to find out how you can make yellow or orange appear as bright as possible.

Light inside

A light in a window is not a reflection, but an actual source of illumination. You can see parts of the room and its furnishings. The important thing is to correlate colors, forms, sizes, values. Don't paint every detail in a 2″ window seen from a distance of two hundred feet. You have to decide what role the lighted window is to play in your picture. Is it to be the main theme? Or is it to be just a little touch of no significance? If it's the main subject, make it larger; it can still be an outdoor painting: an indoor scene painted from the outside, showing the outside of the house, with some vegetation. Observe the reflections of the indoor light on outdoor objects, such as the foliage of a tree, or the ground outside the window.

Other shiny surfaces

Polished stone, marble, metal ornaments are often found in cities. A suggestion is all you have to make in your painting. Show the sparkling highlights on the chromium parts of cars, for example. A bright reflection in a cityscape can be of help to your picture. Edward Hopper, and other noted artists have painted ordinary store fronts, single houses, gas stations and all imaginable scenes of this kind. There's no reason why you mightn't paint a view of ultra-modern stores with metal and glass fronts.

Single light

A lone streetlamp or a light in the window of a cottage in a vast, silent countryside, or a lighted window in a dark skyscraper may be romantic, but it may also be a kind of old-fashioned cliché. Tastes are different, to be sure, and one man's cliché may be another man's great idea. But professional artists avoid painting the silhouette of a kissing couple in a lighted window; pictures of little cottages with one lighted window, smoke curling from the chimney, and an old woman returning home with a load of firewood, or a man walking home with a scythe on his shoulder.

Avoid clichés, such as a black silhouette of people in a lighted window. Observe proportions of persons looking out windows.

Reflected light

Reflected light is not the actual light reflected in some very glossy surface, but the usually faint light inside the shadow caused by light thrown into the shadow by an illuminated surface. You can observe reflected lights on all roundish surfaces, on the opposite side from the direct light. You can also observe such reflected lights when using a flashlight. There's a round spot of illumination where the flashlight hits its target; and there are reflected lights caused by this bright round spot in surrounding objects.

When strong sunlight hits part of the sidewalk in front of a wall in the shade, the bright sidewalk is reflected in the shadow. Reflected light is never as bright as direct light, but it's attractive and important pictorially. Observe it and paint it, without exaggeration. My oil painting demonstration of a view of Casablanca shows such reflected lights in the shadows of white buildings. (Please turn to the color section of this book.)

Painting images in mirrors

Painting images in mirrors will hardly occur in outdoor painting. If it does, remember to paint what you see in the mirror, but include the entire mirror in the picture. That's the only way of showing that the image is a reflected one. You might see the outdoors in a mirror in a room. You have to paint at least the part of the room immediately surrounding the mirror. The reflected image will be smaller than reality, according to distance. You can see a vast landscape or a large part of a city in a mirror no bigger than a window, through which you can see the same scene.

Slight distortions are likely even in the finest mirror; and if the mirror is at a slant, compared with the scenery, the reflected image will be considerably foreshortened. Such a painting would be most fascinating to create, but quite difficult as well.

9 Composition in outdoor subjects

IN FINAL EXAMINATIONS I gave in my many art survey courses at The City University of New York, I often asked my students to define the term "composition." Despite full explanations during the semester, quite a few students thought that composition must be a cheap building material, compressed from various ingredients. Others thought it was instrumental music played by orchestras. I am telling you this absurd little story to show how easily words can mislead us unless we know exactly what we're talking about.

Definition of composition

In the fine arts, composition means the organizing or grouping of the various parts of a work of art so as to achieve a unified whole. The implication is that, in a good composition, no part can be changed, moved, or removed without destroying the satisfactory esthetic appearance of the entire work. Some critics even state that there can be only one good composition for any given work. I am sure this is wrong. The same artist might have arranged the same parts in a different, yet equally satisfactory manner. Many artists have executed several versions of the identical subject and, very often, one is as good as any of the others.

Is composition necessary?

Couldn't an artist paint a good picture by depicting whatever he happens to see, without worrying about arranging his subject in form and color? There's no law against doing such a painting, and it can be good in its own way, provided that each item in it is rendered in a satisfactory fashion. I'd accept such a painting as an exercise in textures or forms, but I must declare, without any hesitation, that such a painting would contain no creativity, no esthetic purpose, and thus, it would be no true work of art.

Prehistoric man painted animals and, later, humans, on the walls of his cave with often astounding skill, but those pictures, done one on top of the other, served magical, rather than artistic goals. Real art begins when primitive man first paints what may be called a picture, in which the various elements are correlated. And we do find such pictures in prehistoric times.

Deliberate or intuitive arrangement?

Much in art is basically intuitive, of course, but intuition has to be developed by training, by experience. Even nonobjective or so-called automatic

A City on a Rock by Francisco de Goya (Spanish, 1746–1828), oil on canvas 33″ x 41″. Goya preceded the Impressionists with dashing brush strokes in his sometimes nightmarish pictures. This sarcastic and imaginative painting of houses built on top of a rock so steep that only flying men could possibly live up there—while crowds below the concave rock seem to be baffled—had to be executed in a sketchy manner. How else could the artist have conveyed his idea of a mysterious place, unattainable to the average man? The rock is slightly off-center, and it's made to look more asymmetrical by pushing the highest roof to the left. Bequest of Mrs. H. O. Havemeyer, 1929. The H. O. Havemeyer Collection, The Metropolitan Museum of Art.

artists, who appear to be piling paint upon paint, must do so with some taste and technical skill, if they want to be considered artists. In representational painting, the need for composition is more obvious. Wouldn't it be silly, for instance, to paint a tree so that it completely covers the most attractive part of a house? Or to paint one-half of a human figure on one edge of a picture, and one-half of a tree on the other?

Isn't spontaneity vital to art?

This is a very common question heard among students. According to the dictionary, spontaneity is the quality of acting from natural impulse or tendency, without effort or premeditation; a self-acting, natural process. Now, is it possible to paint without effort and premeditation? I don't think so. There's no art without effort and premeditation. You may get a sudden inspiration, that's true, but painting is not a self-acting process. You have to get your equipment and start painting with your own hands, with your own mind.

A sudden inspiration may lead you to better, fresher results than a great deal of planning, but spontaneousness in painting can never be the impulsive action which causes you to make out a nice check and mail it to the Red Cross, when you see a terrible natural catastrophe on tv. Artists who start painting without thinking usually come up with a picture so poor in proportions, color, and composition that, after a while, they become disgusted and scrape or wipe the painting off the support.

How can we compose outdoor subjects?

It's easy to compose a still life; we can set it up in many ways; we can add something, move or take out some piece, but what about scenery or a city? How can we move or change what we see? It's true that you cannot move a tree, a house, or a mountain in reality, but you can move anything in your imagination, according to esthetic concepts. You can push things up or down, right or left; eliminate one part, push in another part, provided, of course, that the changes fit geographically, seasonally, and artistically. We smile when Shakespeare sets a play *on the rocky shores of Bohemia.* We know Bohemia is a completely landlocked country. We wouldn't smile, we'd roar with laughter, if you painted magnificent palm trees on the rocky shores of Vienna.

Look for the most interesting view

First of all, look around several times, in order to find a view worth painting. I've described the view finder; such a small gadget can be of immense help to you in seeing the countryside in individual pictures, one after the other. Carry a small sketchbook or pad of paper, and make a few sketches in pencil, ballpoint pen, or crayon. Sketching makes you familiar with the whole panorama. If you have enough time, take your sketches home, study them, combine one item from this sketch with items in other sketches before making a final decision about what to paint.

(Left) Startling views of nature don't always look good in pictures. This sight on the road to the Cape of Good Hope was magnificent to the eye, but absurd as a subject for painting because it consists of three jutting-out mountains almost exactly the same in shape and size. (Right) Blasting had to be done on this road and the geological layers of the earth are revealed here and there. This is one of those geological cross-cuts: interesting to see, but monotonous in a painting.

(Left) This modern church in Johannesburg is fascinating, but how can you paint it, unless you do an architectural rendering? It's as symmetrical as a tent, with no pictorial quality. (Right) A group of tall houses all over the place, in Naples. Interesting, but who'd want to paint all those windows? And this isn't a subject you could simplify. You either paint the houses and windows or you don't. One small section of this view might be a better pictorial subject.

If you have no time to go home and work on the project, decide on the spot where the main scenery should be, and add a few other items, make changes, as you go along. More often than not, very little change is necessary to make nature look a little more interesting in the picture by merely shifting a few parts.

Symmetry or asymmetry?

Symmetry prevailed in classic Greek art, due to the meticulous symmetry of Greek architecture. The Romans accepted this symmetry, and it was revived, or continued in the Christian era, through the Renaissance. The Reformation and the Thirty Years' War played havoc with old ideas, and developed an asymmetrical approach to art in the Baroque period. We still continue the asymmetrical composition to a large extent, and Oriental artists also prefer it, independently from the West.

Foreground, background, middleground

In a still life or figure painting, the main subject is in the foreground, and there's a background to establish the location of the main theme. In outdoor painting, spatial relationship is much more important. It isn't enough to have something strong and perhaps attractive in the foreground, and something to indicate the end of the view, such as a mountain range, with nothing but flat terrain between the front and the rear. A middleground is necessary; some objects to lead the eye from the front to the rear and back again.

Let's accentuate the negative

There are unquestionably many ways in which you can create a well-composed picture, and it is so difficult, if not impossible, to say that if you do this or that, your painting will be just right, that it seems easier to explain what not to do than what to do, in reference to composition. I'll try to point out the mistakes most often made by students; I'll try to explain why those mistakes are mistakes and not merely matters of individuality, taste, or artistic freedom.

Here's a set of don'ts

There's no law against symmetry, but don't paint on the right exactly what you have on the left, and don't paint one big figure or form exactly in the center of the support. Such an arrangement looks artificial, lifeless.

Don't paint a sort of over-all design in which everything appears to be of the same importance, as if it were a section of a wallpaper, a repeat picture used on a chintz.

Don't cut objects off at the edges of the support. This would give the effect of a larger painting trimmed off at the edges. A literal cutting-off did occur in one of the world's most famous paintings, Rembrandt's *Sortie of the Guard Company of Captain Frans Banning Cocq*, popularly, and erroneously, called *The Night Watch*. Originally painted for a larger wall, the painting had to be moved to a smaller wall, and had to be cut off all round, causing irreparable damage to the composition.

Don't cover the entire support with one important part of the subject, from edge to edge. Leave a little breathing space to indicate spatial relationship. A house or a huge wave will not look big because you paint it clear across the support. Size has to be implied by proportions as compared with other items in the picture.

Don't divide the composition into left and right, upper or lower half, or into two triangles, by dividing the support diagonally, keeping practically all pictorial features in one half, and leaving the other half quite empty. Such a painting will appear to be unfinished.

Don't exaggerate the difference between what you consider the most important part and the rest of your subject. You're not painting a poster advertising something.

Don't place big or tall objects close to either side of the support. Such objects will appear to be coming into, or going out of the picture, and make the frame look that much wider on their side of the support.

Don't place objects too close to the top of the support, because such objects seem to be flying away. Naturally, birds or flying machines should be painted up there, but not trees, plants, figures.

Don't place objects too close to the bottom because they will seem to be sinking or dropping out of the picture. It's reasonable, of course, to paint shrubs, rocks, and so forth at the bottom.

Don't place the base of a building or of a big tree at the bottom edge of the support, while leaving ample room for the sky above, as this would make the onlooker feel that the picture had slipped down in the frame.

Don't put objects too high up, leaving a lot of empty space at the bottom, as this would cause people to think the painting had slipped upward, for some mysterious reason.

Don't paint everything in the same tone. Lights and darks play an important role in any pictorial composition. If you paint everything in equally light tones, the painting will seem to have been faded, perhaps due to exposure to sunlight. If you paint everything dark, your picture will look as if it had been darkened by age and dirt, or as if it were covered with a dark veil.

Don't paint a tall subject on a low, horizontal support, and vice-versa. The shape of the support should fit the subject. A waterfall practically cries out for a high, vertical support, while a river scene ought to be painted on a long, horizontal support. If you have any doubt, try the subject on a horizontal support and on a vertical one as well.

(Left) A big object close to one side of the support looks lost, and makes the frame appear that much wider there. The symmetry of the big mountain is monotonous. (Right) Move the big object away from the edge, give it a slight slant; and make other items less centered.

(Left) Don't cover the whole support with one subject. The subject won't look big and strong; it'll appear to have been cut out of something much bigger all round. (Right) Leave enough breathing space. This indicates the scale of the subject, while making it more comprehensible as well.

(Left) This scene in Bora-Bora looks small and crowded. (Right) The horizontal support gives the theme more spaciousness, and the trees look more picturesque.

(Left) The sailing ship is much too high up in the picture, and looks tremendous in size, compared with its distance from the shore. (Right) Although the same ship is bigger here, it looks right because it is the main theme, with the water indicated only to show that it's a real sailing ship. It's a close-up view, and details are justified.

(Left) Most of the weight in design and color is in the left half of this scene from Fiji. (Right) The same trees and native house are shown in a more evenly distributed arrangement.

(Left) Construction in Johannesburg: the picture seems top-heavy. (Right) The same subject has more air. You get the feeling that a very big house is being erected.

(Left) Mondello Beach, Sicily. Both sky and beach look empty, and the big, heavy tower on the left is overwhelming. (Right) The same view has a much better distribution of space and forms on a low horizontal support.

Pyramid in Chichen-Itzá, is either in the center, or too far left or right. Off-center, the pyramid looks more impressive, and the trees give it a feeling of distance.

(Left) A Tunisian street as it really is. Interesting enough, but rather empty. (Right) Placing the same subject lower eliminates the empty space of the street; inclusion of a mosque from another section of the city gives the view much more variety and a better composition. The artist isn't a camera; he may make changes.

(Left) The Casbah in Algiers on a horizontal support doesn't suggest the crowdedness of narrow, winding streets and stairways of this old inner city. (Right) The tall, upright support gives a feeling of narrowness. You feel you cannot avoid rubbing against masses of people.

Photographs of the same corner in New York City, in upright and horizontal positions. Either shape is acceptable; the question is what you'd like to emphasize: the tall houses or the heavy traffic?

(Left) Street in Dakar: perspective is too strong, it looks as if the city were going uphill. (Right) Viewing the same street from a lower eye level fills the entire support with pictorial elements.

(Left) Fishing village in Morocco may be fascinating to see, but leaves large empty spaces in picture. (Right) Selecting a smaller, but more complex part of the actual view, without changing anything, gives a more dynamic picture.

(Left) Two unusual houses don't make a pictorial subject. (Right) The same houses, with trees pulled there from the next block, and a few figures, are now picturesque enough.

(Left) The trees are overpowering and too symmetrical. (Right) I pushed the trees slightly to the right and included the top of the foliage. This gives a more pleasing view.

(Left) Castle on the Rhine: hill and ruins are too high. (Right) The same subject is now too low, with a big empty sky.

(Left) On a horizontal support, the same subject seems more natural. (Right) A lower horizontal support gives the composition an even better balance. The ruins of the castle become an integral part of the whole setting.

(Left) African forest placed too high. The lower half of the picture is flat and empty, and cuts the forest off, makes it appear to be very unimportant. (Right) Covering the entire support with the forest causes the onlooker to realize that this is a wilderness.

High level or low level?

The higher up you are, the broader the view. It depends upon the subject and your own concept from which viewpoint you do an outdoor painting. The ocean is vast, no matter how you look at it. You may want to emphasize the waves, with less space for the sky. Or you may consider the cloudy sky more important than the waves. In cityscapes, a better over-all view is possible from a higher level, but a more detailed painting may require that you look at the city from the street level. The decision is up to you.

Changes in composition

Except for transparent watercolor, in which drastic changes are literally out of the question, you can, and should make corrections or changes in your composition if you find them necessary. Don't continue the painting if you suddenly realize that something is basically wrong, but don't wipe or scrape the paint off without giving the changes careful consideration. It's all right for you to be sorry that you'd gone ahead with the painting without sufficient planning. Don't make things worse by changing your layout too quickly.

Use a plastic or acetate overlay

Many experienced artists attach a sheet of glass-clear acetate to an unsatisfactory painting, and try out the changes on this sheet before deciding what, if anything, they can alter in the painting itself. This simple method can save you a great deal of trouble and disappointment.

What about imagination?

Landscape is often combined with imagination. The scenery may be quite realistic, but peopled with fantastic figures; dreamlike or nightmarish elements are mixed with completely normal, often extremely beautiful sections. The principles of composition are the same as in perfectly realistic renderings of landscapes, marines, or cityscapes.

Moonlight Fantasy, oil on gesso panel 16″ x 20″. Chaos, tidal waves, turbulent clouds are here composed into a fantastic view. A city of skyscrapers, illuminated by the full moon and by unseen lights, is shown against the dark silhouettes of huge waves, rock formations, and a turreted castle. I executed this painting with many glazes in bluish, greenish tones, contrasting with the glowing lights in the city and in the spiraling snake-like clouds. The view is asymmetrical.

10 Color mixing in every medium

EVEN CHILDREN KNOW ABOUT THE PRIMARY COLORS—red, yellow, and blue—and how to mix orange from red and yellow, green from blue and yellow, violet from red and blue. Some kids know that orange, green, and violet are called secondary colors. Few, if any of them hear about tertiary colors which are obtained by mixing any two of the secondary colors with each other. The tertiary colors appear to be just different shades of brown.

Color mixing is an art

For painters, color mixing isn't as simple as this. They soon discover that we need two fundamentally different reds: vermilion (cadmium red), and crimson (alizarin crimson) ; at least two very different yellows: light yellow and medium yellow; and at least three different blues: cobalt, ultramarine, and phthalo (phthalocyanine). Phthalo blue takes the place of Prussian blue, which should not be used because it's too powerful and darkens every color with which it's mixed.

The most startling differences between colors become evident in the mixing. Mix the reds, yellows, and blues with white; mix reds and blues with yellows; mix the reds with blues—the resulting hues will be dramatically different. By mixing more and more mixtures with each other, an artist can obtain any hue and shade he desires. It should be stated here that white is rejected by purists in transparent watercolor, while black is rejected by some artists on the old basis of the scientific concept in physics that black is the absence of all colors. The painter isn't a physicist. To him, black is black, just as green is green.

Develop your sense of color

Color sense in normal eyes can be developed. As a matter of fact, most art students begin to realize what color sense means as soon as their attention is called to this important feature in the art of painting. Generally, people think of colors in reference to the names of colors only. Light blue, dark blue, light red, dark red, chocolate brown, white, off-white, and so forth. For an artist, such names are virtually meaningless, because even chocolate is produced in various shades of brown.

If you want to redecorate a room, you mix a certain color and apply it, with roller or brush, as evenly as possible, and you make sure you've enough paint for the entire job. In a painting, however, hardly any two brush strokes are the same in hue. We say a distant mountain is pale blue, but, after studying it we find many shades of blue, greenish, reddish, grayish, in the same mountain. A house may be built of yellow brick, but the walls don't look one flat yellow all over.

What you don't know does hurt

What you don't know is exactly what hurts you in the final accounting. What you know can only help. Quite a few of my college art students have said to me: "Please don't tell me anything. Let me find out for myself. It may take a little time, but I'll get there much better if you don't interfere." Some of them said this many years ago . . . and they're still trying to get there on their own.

Warm and cool colors

We speak of warm and cool colors. The division is more important than it sounds. A painting executed entirely in warm, or entirely in cool colors is usually dull, like a cheap color postcard, in which either the blues or the reds predominate. Or it resembles a faded color picture. Cool and warm colors have to be juxtaposed in order to achieve interesting results.

Yellow, orange, red, burnt sienna—hues reminding one of fire and flame—are called warm colors. Cool colors, such as white, blue, green, and many colors mixed with white, remind you of cold, ice, snow. Warm colors can be cooled off, so to speak, by adding a little white, blue and/or green to them. Even the "hottest" cadmium red becomes cool when mixed with a drop of white and half a drop of blue. Cool colors can be made warm by adding a drop of red, orange, burnt sienna, yellow. We even have a warm black and a cool black.

Are colors mixed the same way in all media?

Yes, colors are mixed in the same way in all media with three exceptions. Exception No. 1: in transparent watercolor (aquarelle), we use no white for making colors lighter, but either buy a lighter shade of the color, or thin it down with water. Exception No. 2: mixing in pastel should be reduced to the minimum, because rubbing destroys the teeth, the texture of the support. It's advisable to have many shades of pastels and to work with the right shade, instead of relying on mixtures. Exception No. 3: the superimposition of one color over another in felt brush pen is not going to give you a subtle shade, but merely an approximate one. You can make a color darker, but not lighter and, certainly, not brighter. All other painting media mix in the same manner.

How to make colors lighter

White makes colors lighter, but it also makes them cooler and too much white causes a "chalky" appearance. To avoid this, mix the color you wish to make lighter with another light hue, adding a little white if necessary. The light hue, naturally, has to be a member of the same color family. Add yellow to green, to red, to orange, to ocher, to brown; add orange to red, to brown. But you cannot make blue lighter by mixing it with yellow or orange.

White turns alizarin crimson into pink, cadmium red into what we call peach color. Blue or violet can only be lightened with white. In many cases, you have to add a drop of white to the lighter hue. Experiment; make your own chart of mixtures on a strip of support. There's no definite chart in the fine arts as there is in selecting the right shade for your bathroom or kitchen.

The proof is in the painting

Although we usually begin mixing on the palette, it's impossible to judge the correctness of the shade until you apply it to the support, where you can compare it with the surrounding colors. Every color is affected by the colors next to it. A certain yellow may look dull against white, but brilliant against blue or violet.

How to make colors darker

To make colors darker, add darker hues: black and alizarin crimson to blue and green; blue and a dash of black to green and red; burnt sienna to ocher; burnt sienna and red to orange; blue and red to purple. Always a drop only, or just a touch with a corner of the brush. Never prepare a big batch of any shade. Mixing ought to be done stroke after stroke.

How to mix sky-blue

The sky is likely to play a big part in outdoor pictures. Most beginners find it difficult to get a sky-blue. That's because, almost invariably, they start by applying a batch of dark blue and try to lighten it by adding white. First of all, there's the question of which blue to employ? Assuming that you have cobalt, ultramarine, and phthalo blue, try to mix each of these with white. You'll be surprised to find what a difference the blue makes. Ultramarine blue with white looks almost violet next to cobalt blue with white.

Furthermore, a great deal of white can be made light blue with a couple of drops of blue color. Start with white, and add blue gradually. I find phthalo blue the best for a bright, sunny sky; cobalt and/or ultramarine blue should be used in painting seas or lakes and distant mountains. Don't paint the entire sky in the same shade of blue. There are differences even in the sky. The bottom is always a little lighter; often pinkish or yellowish in tone. In watercolor, you have to apply the sky with very wet, thin washes. In other media, try to apply them in the correct shades at once, without going over them again, if at all possible.

Start light mixtures with the lightest hue

What's true for the sky is true for all light colors. Always begin with the lightest ingredient and add the darker tones gradually. You'll find this advice especially valuable in certain light hues, such as yellow, which are amazingly powerful in painting. A very small amount of yellow goes a very long way.

Start dark mixtures with the darkest hue

In dark shades, the procedure is the reverse: begin with the darkest ingredient; add lighter colors gradually. If you start with a light tone, you'll find it difficult and time-consuming to make it sufficiently dark. In the process of adding more and more paint, you often muddy your painting and, ultimately you may find it necessary to wipe or scrape it off.

How to mix violet

Theoretically, red and blue give us violet. You'll soon find that only alizarin crimson and cobalt or phthalo blue can be mixed into violet and always with a little white added. Cadmium red and any of the blues, will give you a kind of brown or maroon, not violet. You can obtain an infinite number of violet shades by varying the comparative quantities of red, blue, and white in the mixture. Violet is an extremely sensitive color, in any medium. Your brush, the colors, and whatever medium you may use—water, linseed oil, turpentine—have to be absolutely clean. The slightest amount of dirt destroys the brilliance of violet, which is a most important color. Something between warm and cool, violet is a hue which goes well with practically any other color.

Small or big palette?

The question about palette refers to the number of colors an artist uses, not to the geometric size of the gadget on which he arranges his paints. A small palette implies that an artist works with few colors; some artists like to have a big palette, that is, a great many different colors. There's also an average palette, used by most experienced artists. In past ages, artists were restricted to whatever pigments they could obtain in their parts of the world. Today, any number of colors can be purchased in any country.

El Greco and Rembrandt are thought to have employed about six colors each, but Leonardo da Vinci worked with a dozen. Even in the past, the number of colors depended upon the individual artist to a certain extent. I know present-day artists who preach the use of six colors only, but I find that their paintings are almost invariably dull and faded-looking. I see no good reason for restricting oneself to a specific number of paints. Buy all you like, but it's literally impossible to use a great many. Where would you keep them? You'd have to have a palette (I mean a palette for your paints), as big as your studio, and you'd have to have a huge space for keeping all those colors. I believe in common sense. Use the really needed colors, from which all other shades can be mixed. I'll give you a list of recommended colors for each medium in the respective chapters.

Do we need mixing mediums?

In watermedia, add water, as much as necessary, no more and no less. In oil painting, add a drop of linseed oil or turpentine only if the paints happen to be sticky, stiff. Never make them run. Retain the original consistency of the paints.

What about glazes and washes?

While basic mixing is necessary, you can obtain outstanding results by going over one color with another color, thinned down either with water, in the watermedia, or with a glazing medium in oil painting. In transparent watercolor, practically the whole painting ought to be executed in washes, one on top of the other. But in casein, polymer, and oil painting, washes or glazes also create a translucent, deep effect, often far superior to ordinary mixing. For example, go over cobalt blue with an alizarin crimson wash or glaze, and the result will be a lovelier violet than if you had just mixed it out of alizarin crimson and blue. Glazing or washes lend every color an enamel-like quality, preferred by the old masters, often neglected by present-day artists. The technique is available to anyone and I recommend that you try it, but glazing requires skill, care, and patience, too.

Haere-Mai by Paul Gauguin (French, 1848–1903), oil on burlap 28″ x 36″. Gauguin spent many years in the South Sea Islands, where he found endless inspiration in the colorfully saronged natives as well as the magnificent scenery, and what he rightly or erroneously believed to be the local, ancient religious rites. Imbued with the concepts of the Impressionists, Gauguin painted vivid, but drastically simplified pictures in colors which seemed impossible to his contemporaries in Paris. Yet, those colors were basically true. Gauguin was aware of Cézanne's strong ideas about careful composition. Collection, J. K. Thannhauser, New York. By Courtesy of Thannhauser Foundation.

11 Painting techniques

CERTAIN ARTISTS SAY there are as many techniques in painting as there are artists. This may be true, but all individual differences are based on the same well-established principles. Every professional musician plays his instrument in fundamentally the same fashion. He sits or stands, moves his hands, fingers, arms, shoulders according to traditional training. He wouldn't dream of rearranging strings or keys of his instrument, with the remark that an artist should do things in his own individual manner. Yet every accomplished musician has his own, personal style which shines through the music he plays.

Painters and their instruments

Painters, too, have to learn the traditional ways of handling their instruments, tools and materials, before they're ready to express their individual concepts. Many, if not all, unsuccessful artists ought to realize that there's a considerable difference between the attitudes of professional artists and art students or amateurs.

How to stand or sit

A large percentage of art students sit or stand the wrong way. For example, a student sets up an easel with a support, and turns in the opposite direction from what he wants to paint. Many are facing at a ninety-degree angle from the subject. This means that they have to turn their heads all the way to the left or right, or all the way round, to see the subject, and then turn their heads back, completely or at a ninety-degree angle, to put on the support what they had just observed. Still other students cover the subject with the support on the easel so fully that they have to peek, right or left, or even above the support, in order to see what they're trying to depict.

All this makes looking, observing, remembering, and painting that much more difficult. The idea is to stand or sit, and to set up your support, in such a fashion that you have a full view of the subject, be it a figure, a still life, or an outdoor scene. If you're right-handed, keep your support on the right; if you're left-handed, keep it on your left. This position enables you to look at the subject and your painting by merely moving your eyes from left to right, or from right to left, without turning your whole head and neck.

Have all your tools and materials in a position where you can pick up what you need without hunting for it. Outdoors or indoors, a few minutes spent on careful and practical arrangement is time well spent.

Mountains at Saint Rémy by Vincent van Gogh (Dutch, 1853–1890), oil on canvas 29″ x 37″. Done during the last year of his life. Contrary to popular belief, Vincent had a great deal of academic knowledge. His contemporaries mistook his epileptic fits for madness, and deprecated the long, swirling brush strokes with which he worked. Every object he painted in this manner seemed to be alive and in motion. He learned much from Gauguin, and, to the very end, he alternated paintings in those swirling, characteristic strokes with others done in the most traditional technique. Collection, J. K. Thannhauser, New York. By Courtesy of Thannhauser Foundation.

Your palette is part of you

The palette shouldn't be a dumping ground for paints of every sort, all messed up. It's as important to the painter as the little black bag is for the physician. The time seems to be past when artists held huge, curved palettes on their arms, with a thumb in the thumbhole. That kind of palette was heavy and the pressure caused the painter's arm to become numb. Most of us now use smaller palettes, and place them on stools, or taborets. I've made a simple attachment for my solid studio easel. Two 1"-wide lattice strips, 12" long, are screwed to the underside of the movable shelf on which my support stands, and on which there's room for brushes. The two strips swivel on the screws. I push them under the shelf, or turn them outward. They're about 8" apart, and I place my palette on these two strips.

Orderliness won't destroy artistry

Any good craftsman has a system; he knows how to organize his work in the most practical manner. Painters ought to start by organizing their palettes. Place your colors on the palette in a systematic fashion, always the same way. The batches of paint should be near the top and on one short side, about an inch from the edge of the palette, not all over the place. And the sequence of colors ought to be reasonable. I place white in the center, warm colors on the left, cool colors on the right. The order is the same, year after year. This is important for two reasons. One, you can find the right color without hunting for it. Two, several colors look equally dark on the palette; for instance, alizarin crimson, ultramarine blue, phthalo green, and black can only be distinguished when mixed with some other colors. I know which is which by keeping them in the same spots.

How to apply paint

In realistic art, we apply paint mostly with brushes, but painting knives are often employed for larger surfaces and certain technical effects. Work with the tool which fits the subject. Don't try to paint a small painting with a big knife or a huge brush.

How to hold the brush

The brush is neither a dagger nor a sledge hammer. Hold it gently, in such a manner that you can twist, twirl, or turn it with ease. Don't rub it hard on one side all the time, as this will turn it into a triangular brush and ruin it very quickly. Keep turning the brush from one side to the other. Don't use a brush as if it were a broom, and don't use it mechanically, in one-and-the-same direction. Slanting brush strokes create the illusion of a wind-blown rainfall; vertical strokes look as if the scene represented a heavy downpour; horizontal strokes give an impression of water; alternating vertical and horizontal strokes resemble a sort of basket weave or floormat. Such strokes are all right, of course, if they are applied deliberately to cause their respective effects.

(Extreme Left) Paint applied in parallel, vertical strokes creates the impression of a pouring rain, or some article made of vertical slots. (Center Left) All horizontal strokes look like water or something made of slots, like a wooden shutter. (Center Right) Slanting, parallel strokes appear to be wind-blown rain. (Extreme Right) Alternating, short, horizontal and vertical strokes seem to simulate an Oriental floor mat, or a basket weave.

Parallel strokes of even lengths are applied by beginners whose aim is to create a feeling of smoothness, as if they were painting a wall, trying to avoid streakiness. For a true over-all effect in fine arts painting, wield the brush in every possible direction, using uneven strokes, overlapping each other, blending them a little by pulling the brush, flat, across the painted section, once in a while.

Clouds, waves, tree bark, applied in impasto. The paint itself is thick enough to indicate a certain material or texture. Make impasto thicker gradually, instead of piling the paint up in huge heaps at once.

Achieving an over-all effect

Wield your brush in every possible direction, with uneven, overlapping strokes, without leaving ridges of paint between strokes. Add a little of this and that color, constantly, in order to vary the shades. No large surface ever looks exactly the same from one end to the other, from top to bottom. There must be differences in shades. If you work in the suggested manner, the result will be an over-all effect, without disturbing monotony. This kind of application refers to oils, polymer, and casein.

What about aquarelle?

In transparent watercolor, we work with plenty of water, in more or less wet washes which spread all over the paper. You have to watch the colors all the time: keep them from running too far, or from drying with strong rings that can never be eliminated. Brush strokes are normally not discernible in aquarelle.

Applying pastel

Although pastels are applied in strokes, the colors ought to be rubbed around immediately with fingertips or stumps. Unrubbed strokes or lines remain noticeable through the finished pastel picture and may look like strange flaws in the support.

Impasto

The heavy application of paint, called *impasto,* is quite popular with the public as well as the artist. I sometimes suspect that lay people purchase impasto paintings because they think they're getting their money's worth in paint. Impasto is feasible in oils and polymer. Don't try it in casein or in aquarelle as the thick paint will crack off very soon. Impasto may be done entirely in paint, but there are certain very good substances which help you apply impasto.

Gel

A gelatinous substance (hence the name) has been used in oil painting for several generations, but it often caused darkening and cracking. Now, gel is prepared with scientific care, so that anyone might use it without fear. There's gel for oils and gel for polymer. Don't mix them up! This vaseline-like medium gives all colors a quality of transparency without reducing their brightness and without altering their viscosity. Gel is usually mixed with the paint, but it may be applied directly, and painted afterward.

Extender or modeling paste

A new material, made to be used with polymer, extender, or modeling paste is good for any medium if you apply it as it is, and paint over it when dry.

You can mix it directly with polymer paints. At first, this paste was made of white marble dust; now, it's also prepared from pulverized asbestos. The effect is the same, but asbestos is considerably lighter than marble, and a lightweight support may be used for it. Still, I prefer to do impasto on a strong support, such as Masonite, multimedia board, wood panel, or canvas board, not on paper or stretched canvas.

Build up the extender to any thickness, but do it gradually, and give each application a chance to dry before adding another heap. This method is recommended in any type of impasto. Huge batches of paint or paste won't dry inside for quite some time, and are likely to cause some damage. Someone might prick a heap of such paint or paste and the inside will splurt out.

Polymer gesso

This is a preparation for priming supports, as we do in oil painting, but the polymer gesso is water-based and dries very fast, so that you can paint over it immediately. The gesso may also be used in building up impasto, but the extender is better, especially for more intricate forms. Oils may be painted over polymer gesso, but polymer won't adhere to oil gesso. Gel, extender, or gesso may be applied with brush, knife, spoon, toothbrush, tongue-depressor, or even with a cake-decorator.

Underpainting white

Most major manufacturers produce underpainting or texture whites. These come in tubes and look like regular white paint, but dry faster and retain any shape into which you form them. Mixed with other colors, underpainting white causes them to dry faster, according to the amount of this white in the mixture. In all these and other new, or unfamiliar media, read the instructions on the labels, and do yourself a great favor: use only as directed.

Blending colors

Blending seems to be a magic word. Practically every student asks the instructor: "How do I blend colors?" The answer is: apply the right colors in the right values to the right places first, then blend them with brushes or with your fingertips until you achieve the desired appearance of smoothness. You have to try this, in order to find out how much paint you have to apply, and how wet the colors should be while you blend them. If they're too wet, the paints run into each other and create streaks; if they're dry, you cannot blend them at all. Generally speaking, a softer brush is recommended for blending and the brush has to be wiped clean several times during the process.

Watch the results

There's no prescription for technical matters. You have to experiment, and observe the results. Blending oils is the easiest as oil colors remain wet for a couple of days or longer. Casein and polymer dry very fast. You have to keep them wet by adding a little water, or blend the colors immediately. You can also achieve the effect of softness by applying lighter and darker shades directly, without trying to blend paints already on the support.

Is blending necessary?

In fashionable portraits, and figure painting, smooth blending is often desirable. In other subjects, it may be better to avoid slickness. Some parts or phenomena of nature may require softness, such as clouds, but most outdoor items look better when left crisp and fresh. I've seen artists paint big rocks which looked like dark pillows, rather than the hard, strong substance they really are.

Watch other artists at work

There are demonstrations in schools, art exhibitions, art workshops all over the country. Experienced artists show how they work in diverse media. Make every effort at attending such demonstrations. Instrumentalists watch accomplished musicians at concerts, to find out just how they sit or stand, how they manipulate their respective instruments. Painters ought to be just as interested in the technical approach of other painters. You cannot live long enough to find things out for yourself.

When is a painting finished?

This is an important question. The answer depends upon subject, style, the artist's standard of art, his personality, and the element of time. A sketchy painting is often better than a finished one. Or, at least, we accept errors in a sketch we wouldn't accept in a finished work. In general, I'd say a painting is finished when you see nothing else you could add to it or do with it. It's quite possible that a painting which appears to be finished to you today, will appear to be crudely unfinished when you look at it a year or two later.

Stop working when you feel you'd done all you could. You might look at your work at home, in a week or so, and perhaps find a few rough spots to eliminate. One thing is sure, though. The painting should be carried to the same level of execution all over the support. Don't go into full detail in one section, leaving the rest unfinished. If the time you can spend on a picture is restricted, begin with that in mind, and try to create a satisfactory over-all effect.

Grand Canal, Venice by Joseph Mallord William Turner (English, 1775–1851), oil on canvas 36″ x 48⅛″. The sketchiness of this work, a shock to Turner's contemporaries, is reminiscent of El Greco's *View of Toledo.* Although the picture is a flat scene, observed from a gondola, it has tremendous depth. The tallest masts are not in the center, and the shore view is carefully selected in such a fashion that the piazza and the steps leading to the church on the right offer a nice contrast to the houses built straight out of the Grand Canal on the left. Emphasis is on color, motion, and atmosphere, not on small detail. Bequest Cornelius Vanderbilt, 1899. The Metropolitan Museum of Art.

12 Figures and objects, still and in motion

Natural scenery and seascapes can well exist without human beings. Cities may seem to be deserted at certain times of the day or week. Streets are literally empty during siesta time in Southern European and North African cities. Houses can be painted from the second floor up, without showing pedestrians and vehicles. Sooner or later, though, you'll be up against the problem of painting figures and man-made objects.

Man-made objects

Carriages, cars, trucks, buses, trains, planes, bicycles are all over our streets and roads. There are boats on water. You'll see demolition or construction machinery everywhere. All these may be standing still, or be in motion. In many cases, they're not only intimately connected with the subject, but constitute the main theme.

Painting vehicles

You cannot paint any vehicle, old or new, without understanding its construction, its basic perspective. Don't worry about decorations and small details, but do observe the main forms. Draw sketches or study photographs before including any vehicle in your painting; don't make the vehicle more exactly than the rest of the subject.

Painting boats

Boats range from kayaks through sailboats to huge ocean-going vessels and streamlined Diesel ships. Here, too, a fundamental understanding is necessary, and the diversity of marine subjects is so great that you have to specialize in one field or another. My advice is that you include boats or ships in your seascapes only as accessories, preferably in the distance, so as not to necessitate correct details. Observe the general shape, proportions, colors, and values of such ships. A black ship isn't jet black when it's twenty miles off-shore; it's just a medium gray.

Boats close to shore

Make very good sketches or study photographs, and make sure to use the entire combination as you find it. Don't try to combine a boat from one picture with a wharf from another picture, and a shore from still another picture. The chances are that the combination will give the most absurd perspective.

Is precise rendering necessary?

Don't go beyond your usual level of execution in details or accessories, but if you're in the habit of depicting small details in houses, you'll have to do the same in other parts of your subject. Today, representational artists are normally satisfied with an impressionist effect. Andrew Wyeth and his followers go into minute detail in every part of their paintings. Whatever your style may be, stick to it all over the picture.

Painting moving vehicles

In posters, and advertising illustrations, we usually indicate motion with what we call "speed-lines"—little horizontal or slightly slanting lines drawn in the opposite direction, thus suggesting a dash or flight forward. We cannot very well do this in a fine arts painting, but we can slightly blur objects in motion. The Futurists, early in the twentieth century, showed motion by repeating the actions of legs, arms, bodies, wheels, over and over again, one overlapping the other. The idea was followed later in photography, when many pictures of a moving figure were snapped on the same negative within one second or less.

Painting boats in motion

Boats and ships in the distance hardly seem to move; such vessels should be painted small, in very faint hues. Bigger ships, nearer to the onlooker, visibly split the waves with their prows, and waves fan out from their sterns, especially in ships with propellers. Such waves are ample indication of motion. Sailing ships have characteristic slants in their masts, besides billowing sails. Note that the flags and smoke are always blown in the same direction as the sails.

Painting bicycles and motorcycles

In American cities, such conveyances are not very numerous. In many European countries, however, the number of bicycles is astronomical. A typical scene from such places is bound to contain bicycles. Study them, their sizes, proportions, the way they look from various angles, before adding them to your paintings.

Painting mechanical equipment

In the hands of an artist, the most intricate or terrifying mechanical contraption becomes an esthetic subject, but you have to know what it is, how it functions. Many artists love demolition themes, when the walls of formerly very private apartments become visible to all passers-by. You can see the wallpaper, or the painted walls, on floor upon floor, and the traces of former floors and ceilings, stairs, corridors. It's a colorful subject which goes well with big cranes, digging and hoisting machinery. Make careful studies before attempting such a scene.

Make sketches of anything that can ever be included in paintings: cars, boats, machinery, even a hot dog stand.

Figures in outdoor pictures

The inclusion of figures contributes to the salability of paintings. Some of our painters, especially aquarellists, overpopulate their cityscapes. One figure is sitting on a porch; another is asleep on a bench; one is reading a newspaper, while two others talk to each other on a stone step. People look out windows, shake blankets, sprinkle flowers. Such pictures are in the family of *genre,* that is, story-telling conversation pieces. However, an Oriental or African bazaar or market cannot exist without lots of people. Since figures aren't the main features in an outdoor scene, but just accessories, consider the following points:

1. Paint the figures in proportion to the settings.

2. Show groups, rather than individual figures.

3. Place figures only where they naturally belong.

4. Make them stand, sit, or act the way real people would in the circumstances.

5. Paint the figures in the same style as the rest of the picture.

6. Make sure the figures appear to be properly dressed, even though you're not going into fine details. Farmers generally don't dress like city slickers; women in various countries wear different colors and costumes. There's great variety in apparel and colors in a Western city, but, in the Far East, people may dress very much alike, almost in a sort of civilian uniform. Give only a vague idea of these or similar facts in your painting, but don't neglect the necessary observation or research.

Anatomy of humans

You needn't know much about human anatomy for such small figures, but you ought to know how people walk, run, gesticulate, sit, or stand. Take photographs. Buy a small manikin with movable parts, or acquire a group of plastic stick-figures which can be twisted or turned in every imaginable manner. But be careful: turn or twist them in a natural fashion. A plastic manikin might run backward; a real person couldn't.

Avoid being ridiculous

Not every artist can paint figures, just as not every artist can paint portraits or seascapes. Some very famous portrait painters were unable to paint full figures; others were unable to paint a scenic background. Claude Lorrain (1600–1682), whose real name was Claude Gelée, probably the most popular of all French artists of his time, painted fabulous, idealized scenery with Roman and Greek palaces and ruins. But he was unable to paint the mythological, historical, biblical figures much in demand at the time, so he had other artists, especially Courtois and Filippo Lauri, do the figures. He used to say he was selling only his landscapes, and he was giving away the figures.

Don't force yourself to paint figures if you're weak in the field. It's better not to paint them at all than to paint them in a childish fashion. Or make a suggestion of a figure, rather than a detailed form.

Painting groups or crowds

Apply strokes of diverse colors suggesting the torsos: jackets, blouses, shirts; add strokes indicating legs, arms, skirts, pants; paint spots of ocher or pink for faces and dark spots representing heads seen from the back. Spots of diverse colors for hats, in a place where hats are worn. Consider proportions and motion, but no detail. Not all people are of the same height and go in the same direction. Think of all this while painting and the results will be satisfactory. Overlap figures, of course; don't paint them as if they were marching soldiers.

Individual figures

If you have to paint one figure or just a couple of figures, you have to be more precise, but without going into primitive details, unless you wish to emulate Grandma Moses or Henri Rousseau. I suggest that you make sketches and study photographs, and possibly draw such figures on a tracing paper first, and try them out "for size" on the painting when the rest is practically finished. Study especially Impressionist paintings; see how those artists rendered people. A suggestion of shape, motion, clothing is normally necessary, but no eyes, eyebrows and nostrils, please, on a ¼" or ½" head! Simplification can hardly be as dangerous as elaboration. A sketchy approach looks full of life from a short distance; mistakes become obvious in too much detail.

Painting animals

Although you recognize cats and dogs, horses and burros, that doesn't mean you can paint them. Before you paint any animal, no matter how small in size, make a thorough study of that animal. Pictures are always available, if you have no way of studying animals directly. Observe their proportions, heads, ears, horns, if any; and, above all, observe the way they walk, the way their legs move. It's much better to copy animals from good photographs than to try to paint them from a vague memory.

Painting vehicular traffic

Most cities have plenty of traffic and it's better to paint heavy traffic than just a solitary automobile, unless you want to make a point of painting just one car in an otherwise desolate or deserted place. Observe traffic. Look at the variety of cars and trucks—variety in shapes, sizes, colors. Don't paint them all from the same side, but as they are in reality, coming and going. If you're looking down from an upper story, you see the tops of cars. If you're standing on the side, you view them from an angle. Make sketches of diverse vehicles from various angles, and suggest only their main shapes and proportions, instead of trying to depict their chromium fixtures.

It may seem ridiculous to mention this, but it's true that traffic is right-handed in most Western countries, left-handed in many Far Eastern places. As long as you're working in a representational style, you might as well observe on what side the traffic runs in a particular city. You won't get a traffic ticket if you paint a car driving on the right in Great Britain or India, but people familiar with such countries will surely think there's something wrong with your picture.

Observe values

Once again, I mention values. The position of any color between white and black should always be determined. Whether you paint mechanical gadgets, animals or humans, cars or boats, make sure they're not too dark or too light. A ship painted black on the horizon looks like a hole in the support. A sail painted bright white in the far distance looks like a piece of paper stuck onto the picture by some accident. People and cars in the distance may be in various hues, but all of them have to be lighter and hazier than people and cars in the foreground.

Sketch individual figures or groups, crowds, wherever you are. These sketches are from North African market places and streets.

In painting crowds, first apply strokes suggesting the bodies (coats, jackets, blouses) of people, in a variety of colors characteristic of the place and the season. Next, add more torsos, then legs, skirts, also in the proper colors. Add still more overlapping strokes, but begin to add heads: dark spots for hair, light spots for faces, colors for hats and caps. Consider the fact that people are of different heights and not evenly distributed. They aren't all coming toward you, facing you, nor are they all turning their backs on you. Finally, make sure there is variety in density, color, and spatial relationship. Some figures are nearer, others farther away.

13 Photographs are helpful

AROUND THE TURN OF THE TWENTIETH CENTURY, painting from photographs was considered nothing short of reprehensible. It was the same as copying reproductions or picture postcards—something done only by amateurs. A real artist had to work from life, even if it would take him months to finish his work. It was a shock to me when I visited a well-known portrait painter in his studio, and saw him work on a portrait from a large photograph. Being young and outspoken, I asked him if he wasn't cheating. "This is a portrait from life," he declared indignantly. "But I cannot expect a rich lady to come to my studio fifteen times. She couldn't sit still, like a professional model, anyway. So I make up for this by using a photograph which helps me to establish the exact features. But there's much more to art than exact details. Now, I can put more of my own personality into the painting by eliminating a few time-consuming steps."

This statement left a deep impression in me. I realized, in due time, that superficial resemblance, in any subject, isn't what counts. And I know that now, professional artists in all fields use photographs, but they don't actually copy these; they all have sufficient experience in working from life, and the photographs serve largely as foundations on which to build creative, realistic works.

The camera isn't an artist

Don't expect every snapshot to be a picture worth painting just the way it is. The camera is a helpmate. It replaces the kind of sketching Constable and Turner and many other artists had to do before the introduction of photography. You can take many pictures and study them, before selecting a scene for painting. Even then, the chances are that you'll have to combine several photographs in order to obtain a truly satisfactory subject.

Enlarged photographs contain details you could hardly ever have the time to draw by hand, on the spot. Perspective, naturally, is made much easier because the photograph shows everything reduced to a two dimensional, flat surface. Lights and shadows are bound to be correct, since the photograph is taken in less than a second, and thus shows everything in the same light. What you have to consider is how many, or which details are of importance in a painting. The camera has to take a picture of whatever is in front of it. You have to select what you want.

Beware of color photographs

Color photos are very popular because, to the average person, they look more real than black-and-white pictures. For a painter, color photography is acceptable only when done by a first-rate professional photographer. Even then, there are discrepancies between colors in reality and colors in photography. In snapshots, colors are invariably false: too blue or too brown, too yellow or too green; one or another color always comes out in an exaggerated form. We accept this in a photograph, but such discrepancies would "kill" a fine arts painting.

Color slides

Color slides can only be viewed in projectors. The light going through the transparency makes all colors glow like stained-glass windows. This is a beautiful, but totally false effect. Paintings are opaque, not transparent. We say that a certain painting glows with color, but this refers to the comparative brightness of hues. Trying to copy colors in a transparency is hopeless and meaningless.

Color perspective in color snapshots

The camera reduces sizes, but doesn't seem to reduce colors; at least not sufficiently. Distant objects look smaller and hazier as well. This is seldom noticeable in color snapshots. A mountain miles away may be as dark as an object a few feet away. A red roof in the distance is just as bright a red as a similar roof nearby. Color photographs or slides may well be used as guides, to remind you of the colors of certain structures, fields, flowers, clothing, cars, and so forth. With experience, you can change the often overpowering colors in such photographs to the more subtle shades required in fine arts painting.

Make color sketches

Your best bet is to make color sketches by hand, in any medium, without worrying about details, proportions, perspective. Jot down, in color, the darkest and the lightest tones, at least. I often make a pencil or ballpoint sketch and merely write down the colors of important or unusual items. I'll make a note that something is dusty brick color, like my easy chair, green like my shower curtain, red like my folding chair. I add such sketches and notes to clear black-and-white photographs, and have better results than I'd have by working with the help of color snapshots.

Combination of pictures

As with sketches, you can, and usually have to, combine several photographs before finding a stimulating subject. The procedure is identical: take a generally good view, and remove what you don't like, add items you like; move sections one way or another. By tracing some items on clear acetate, you can literally push things around. This is a very good method, employed by quite a few artists. Instead of making changes later, they try everything out in tracings.

Don't copy pictures from travel folders

Paint from photographs made by yourself, even if you take pictures of world-famous views, of which innumerable pictures may be bought in souvenir shops. A photo taken by you is bound to contain something a little different, a personal touch, whereas photographs in travel brochures are all the same, distributed in thousands and thousands of copies. Nothing is more pathetic, in my estimation, than to recognize a typical photograph from an international travel booklet in the painting of a friend . . . who had never even seen the actual place, but merely copied a photograph.

Photographs and atmospheric moods

When working outdoors, you're normally tied down by actual atmospheric conditions—clouds, rain, bright sunlight, early morning, late afternoon—and these conditions will be reflected in your painting. When working from photographs, you can choose your favorite weather or time of day; or the conditions you think would bring out the finest points in your subject. Use the photograph as a foundation, a layout, but paint the colors of your own preferred combination.

You can observe colors in various kinds of weather anywhere, not necessarily where your sketches and photos were made. Rain is the same in Great Britain and New England; twilight and city lights are the same in New York and Cape Town. You can superimpose atmospheric effects on the basis of local observation.

14 Painting outdoors in oils

OIL PAINTING IS STILL THE MOST POPULAR painting medium in the Western world. Artists, art students, and lay people alike seem to believe it represents the highest level of artistry. This is an error of judgment, as artistry doesn't depend upon any medium. The mistake may have at its root the assumption that oils are for adults only, since little children paint with watercolors. People forget, or fail to know, that many of the greatest masterpieces of painting, especially frescoes, were executed in a water medium.

Oils have certain advantages over most painting media. One advantage is that oils can be applied to probably any surface, except fresh plaster, thin paper, and other thin materials. Oil colors are water- and acid-proof. They dry slowly, and allow the artist to make changes by merely scraping or wiping off the paint; or by going over dry paint with any other color.

Equipment for outdoors

For painting outdoors, you'll need a solid paintbox, palette, about fifteen tubes of paint, a palette knife (long, flat blade, for scraping), a painting knife (shorter, trowel-shaped blade), brushes, rags, palette cups; small jar of linseed oil, small jar of turpentine; charcoal sticks; folding easel and stool; a piece of dropcloth on which to keep your stuff from rolling away in grass or weed; a canvas-carrier, so you can take your wet oil painting home without smudging the painting.

Supports

Canvasboard or multimedia board is the most practical support for painting outdoors. Gesso-coated Masonite is also good, but heavier. Stretched canvas is vulnerable: it tears easily if a breeze gets a hold of it. Large sizes are difficult to handle. Indoors, naturally, you may work on any support, in any size.

Recommended list of colors

Alizarin crimson	Yellow ocher	Chromium oxide green
Cadmium red medium	Ultramarine blue	Cobalt violet
Cadmium orange	Cobalt blue	Burnt sienna
Cadmium yellow light	Phthalo blue	Ivory black
Cadmium yellow medium	Phthalo green	Titanium white

Note: Many artists like burnt umber and green earth (terre verte). These colors can be obtained by mixing burnt sienna with black and blue,

Northeaster by Winslow Homer (American, 1836–1910), oil on canvas 34⅜″ x 50¼″ (1895), one of the artist's best-loved paintings. Homer became America's grand master of the sea. He loved water and observed its endless, but rhythmic undulations, and its ever-changing colors. Here, too, off-centered composition prevails. The picture would lose its majestic power if the rock and the huge spray were in the center, rather than on one side or the other. Gift of George A. Hearn, 1910. The Metropolitan Museum of Art.

chromium oxide green with yellow ocher, respectively. Until recent times, flake white and zinc white were the only whites used by artists. Flake white turns dark after a while; zinc white is permanent, but too transparent, without any covering power; titanium is the only white recommended.

Brushes

Most oil painters work with bristle brushes which come in three main types: 1. *Brights,* which have comparatively short bristles, curving slightly inward. 2. *Flats,* which have comparatively long, straight bristles. 3. *Rounds,* which are round in crosscut, but not sharp-pointed. Flats may be best for large surfaces; brights have sharper edges; rounds may be wielded in any direction with the same effect. Try them all, in ¼", ½", and ¾" sizes, and have enough brushes on hand.

I recommend a couple of ½" and ¾" flat red sable brushes and two or three small, round, pointed red sables for finishing touches and signatures. Never use watercolor brushes in oil painting or vice-versa.

Clean oil brushes first by wiping the paint off, then rinsing in turpentine, and washing them in soap and lukewarm water. Keep the handles clean, too. Place clean brushes in a jar, with the handle at the bottom, and don't allow the hairy part to lean against something. If you do, the brush will soon acquire a permanent curvature, and it will be all but useless for painting.

Mediums

Only two mediums are needed outdoors: linseed oil and turpentine, both of artists' quality, not something you buy in a hardware store. If you're allergic to turpentine, an odorless synthetic liquid is available. Use only turpentine for making colors spread a little easier when you begin a painting. Later, add a few drops of linseed oil to the turps. Never use more medium than absolutely necessary. Oil paints ought to be applied as they come from their tubes. Never add any dryer to your paints; it would cause darkening and cracking. If you want to make the colors dry faster, use a little more turpentine.

Layout

Instead of jumping headlong into painting, make a few sketches in pencil, first, to familiarize yourself with the subject. When you're sure you know what you want to paint, make a layout in soft charcoal, indicating the main features of the scene. Use charcoal sticks, not the so-called charcoal pencil, which is difficult to erase. Go over the charcoal layout with a small brush dipped into yellow ocher, thinned down with turpentine, and wipe off the charcoal immediately. Don't worry if the paint smudges a little. The idea of the yellow ocher lines is to eliminate charcoal particles. Some artists make a perfect layout in charcoal and spray it with fixative. I find the ocher outlining quicker and better. And why carry fixative?

How to begin an oil painting

Place a little of every color on your palette at once. Don't think that all you need is green, because you're painting green meadows, trees with green foliage. You need every one of your colors, even if you don't immediately realize this. In an outdoor subject, always start with the background, which is usually the sky, and come forward gradually. The reason is purely technical. As a rule, many items reach into the sky, so to speak: houses, hills, trees, lampposts, and so forth. It would be painstaking, if not literally impossible, to paint such often delicate items first, then try to go round them with the colors of sky and perhaps the colors of distant mountains. The result would resemble cutouts pasted on a support, or stenciled designs.

Paint the sky clear across the section, over the yellow ocher outlines. The outlines bleed through slightly, so that you don't lose your layout. In a landscape, mountains or hills are often in the background. Do these next, also quite completely, going over whatever is in front of them, but allowing the outlines to show through. Try to apply the right colors in the right shades to the right places at once. Of course, it's unlikely that you could do this to perfection; if your color happens to be too dark or too light, or of the wrong shade, correct it immediately, not later.

Students often continue with the wrong color over a large section. They tell me they'll change it afterward. Just when is afterward? To me, afterward is the very moment after I made a mistake. You have to be aware of what you're doing at all times.

As I pointed out in the chapter on color mixing, begin with the lightest color when you need a light shade, and with the darkest when a dark hue is involved. For instance, if it's a cloudy day, begin the sky with white, and add blue or black, gradually, a drop at a time, until the shade is just right. Wield the brush in all directions, rather than scrubbing it on one side all the time.

Coming forward, paint objects without leaving the canvas unpainted anywhere, and don't paint strokes *around* an item, but *into* them, or *away* from them. Strokes or streaks around an object are called "ghosts" because they do resemble ghosts, ectoplasm or something. Remember that there are countless shades in nature; nothing is just one flat color. Don't apply paint in thick strokes until the end. Thick paint dries with ridges and this makes any changing difficult unless you scrape the ridges off.

Changes and corrections

Don't just add more and more paint in oils, because this makes the painting look muddy. Scrape or wipe off the section you wish to change before adding more paint. If very delicate hues are involved, rub the section clean with a little turpentine. Naturally, you can make any change when the colors are dry, but oil colors have a tendency to bleed through, gradually, perhaps in the course of several years. This means that an old painting, or part of an old painting, may become fairly visible, or at least noticeable, through a finished work. It's better to remove the section you don't like than just to paint over it when it's dry.

Blending

As I explained before, blending isn't important in outdoor painting. Better leave the forms a little crisper than too soft. I've seen artists paint a landscape so softly that it looked like a view through misty glass.

Impasto and other textures

As soon as you know where everything is in your picture, impasto—thick applications of paint—may be added. Use brushes for small impasto, painting knife for heavy impasto. Apply the paint in directions and ways simulating natural forms: tree bark in short, ragged, upright strokes; water, waves, ripples, in short horizontal strokes, or big, bold, wavy strokes; clouds may require big swirls. Gel or quick-drying underpainting white will help you in this work. Consider perspective in impasto, too. Don't pile up as much paint in the background as in the foreground.

What about a mahlstick?

The German word *mahlstick* means a painting-stick. Originally, it was any straight stick of wood. Now, it's made of light aluminum in three 10″ sections which can be pushed into each other. It weighs only three-and-a-half ounces. You place one end against the edge of the support, holding the stick at a slant. You can then lean your brush-hand on it, in case you're afraid you might smudge the painting. The mahlstick is used only in oil painting and pastel; other media dry fast enough so that you may lean against the picture whenever necessary.

Retouch varnish

Oil paintings have a tendency to sink in. Dull, grayish spots appear, here and there, damaging the appearance of the painting. Certain artists believe they can avoid this sinking-in if they spray the support with retouch varnish before starting to paint. The simplest method is to spray retouch varnish on the dull spots when the painting is dry to the touch. Apply the varnish with a mouth atomizer or a spray can, never with a brush, and keep the support flat. Otherwise, the varnish might cause some colors to run downward. You'd never apply this varnish outdoors, but you will surely need it at home.

Final varnish

In oil painting, final varnish is highly recommended. It protects the painting and enables someone, perhaps long after your death, to clean the painting by removing the dirty, darkened varnish. Use only artists' picture varnish and read the label with care. Certain artists follow the ill-advised procedure of mixing their paints with a final varnish, in order to obtain a gloss which, in their estimation, will make the painting as good as if it had been actually varnished. Don't do this.

Step one. First, I made a simple layout in charcoal, establishing the main forms and proportions. I went over this with a thin yellow ocher, making sure that the upright lines in the buildings were truly vertical by measuring them from the left or right edge of the support. I wiped the charcoal off so that charcoal dust shouldn't sully the oil colors.

Step two. You have to start outdoor paintings from the background, and come forward gradually. The background is usually the sky. I painted the sky, from the outlines of the houses upward, going over the yellow ocher outlines. The bottom of the sky is almost white; more and more phthalo blue is added as you go upward. I applied colors all over the picture: white in the illuminated parts of houses, bluish or blackish gray in the shadows; a few strokes in the tall minaret, a few bright hues in the awnings, jumping from one spot to another, so as to achieve a fast over-all effect.

OIL DEMONSTRATION 113

Step three. Continuing the same method, I completed
the sky, the walls, the minaret and went into better
definition of shadows all over the picture. The figures
were almost obliterated. You have to paint the street
and the rest before adding the crowds.

Final stage. CASABLANCA CROWD. Details are the last thing to do. I painted windows, shutters, showing that the windows are built into the walls, not just painted upon them. The lights reflected from white walls and roofs into the shadows added much to the interest of the painting. I defined the awnings, the cast shadows on white walls. Then came the figures. No tiny details, such as noses, eyes, ears; only the main shapes and colors, based on good sketches. I indicated Muslim and European garments, turbans. Some figures walk, others stand and talk. I added a bright red spot in the lower left where a man is wearing a fez. Highlights on shoulders and heads help bring the figures to life.

OIL DEMONSTRATION 115

Step one. Working on the heaviest rag-paper, which required no pasting down, I made a simple layout in pencil. I measured the horizon, so it should be absolutely horizontal. A crooked horizon on the ocean is distressing. I indicated only the most important forms.

Step two. Using a 1″ flat sable brush, I covered the sky and the sea with very light, wet washes, leaving the paper white around the promontory, where the waves break into white foam. I also applied a few wet washes on the main shore. As soon as the paper was dry, I erased all pencil marks.

Step three. More washes in the sky, grayish at the bottom, cobalt blue at the top. I added darker blue, green, alizarin crimson washes to the sea; burnt sienna, orange, yellow ocher washes to the rocks; green, ocher washes in different strengths over the vegetation. Here and there, I gave better definition to the rocks, trees, bushes on the shore.

Final stage. CAPE OF GOOD HOPE. I used less water and more paint where sharp forms were necessary, as in the rock formation of the promontory, and some sections on the mainland, but always gradually. I added the individual rocks off-shore in the foaming sea; indicated waves with darker hues. At the end, I painted the cluster of trees in the left foreground. All colors in this feature were strong enough, so that I was able to cover the washes on the section without any difficulty. The last touches were made with a single-edge razor blade: I scratched out a few ripples and whitecaps in the sea, just by pulling a corner of the blade over the top of the paper's texture.

Step one. Just as in oil painting, I made a charcoal layout and went over it with a thin yellow ocher, and wiped the charcoal off. Note that the layout is concerned only with the main forms: hills, street line, wall, the big trees, the shapes and positions of houses, the bigger roofs, windows, and chimneys.

Step two. Starting again with the sky, I painted it over the trees and the outlines of the hills. Such outlines show through the color of the sky sufficiently, so that I was able to go over them with the proper dark colors as soon as the sky was done. Casein dries very fast. I painted the hills, also across the trees, and laid out the main colors in the villas.

Step three. I finished the background and now completed the houses partly covered by the trees. I also began to paint the stone wall at the bottom, suggesting the stone construction by applying spots of paint in diverse hues, such as burnt sienna, ocher, bluish and reddish gray, like mosaics. I also did the trunks and major branches of the trees in black, burnt sienna, and red.

Final stage. VILLAS NEAR CAPE TOWN. This isn't supposed to be an enlarged picture postcard, but a work of art. I went into such details as I considered important: some of the windows and balconies, the more decorative chimneys, branches of trees, the main shapes of the foliage; I painted a few smaller trees in the background; I pulled the stone wall together with a couple of washes (ivory black, alizarin crimson, Payne's gray); I painted the gate in the wall, the cast shadows on the street; added highlights to tree trunks and some sections of the foliage.

Step one. As usual, a simple outline in charcoal was all I needed. It would be a waste of time to draw every single house and window in a picture of this kind. I went over the charcoal with yellow ocher outlines, indicating some of the major trees and out-standing houses. I wiped the charcoal off the support and began to paint.

Step two. I painted the glowing, yellowish white sky below and between the clouds; then the distant mountain, in blue and violet tones, and the hill on the right, closer to me, in more detail. I painted the houses, here and there, in very soft pastel shades of green, yellow, ocher, blue, pink, violet, some white, with reddish roofs; a spot of green, indicating the beautiful cypress trees and the denser vegetation in front.

Step three. I found the clouds too dark and made them lighter; added more differentiation in the nearby hill and in the larger houses, especially the one on the right.

Ralph Fabri

Final stage. VIEW OF TAORMINA. It's a matter of working all over the support, rather than trying to finish one spot at a time. Add a bright touch here, a shadow there; paint a few windows where this enhances the design or the interest, on a bigger wall; define a tree or two. Consider values: nothing in the distance can be as bright as in the foreground. The greens, especially, aren't even green faraway, but bluish. This was a cloudy day, too, so that contrasts between light and shadow aren't very prominent.

Step one. Pastel can only be laid out in pastel, not in pencil or charcoal. I applied a few strokes, including the lower part of the sky, which almost blended into the hills. Note that pastel lines remain visible through superimposed pastel which is rubbed into the support, but rubbed-in pastel can be covered with any other pastel.

Step two. I did the clouds right across the tree branches; then the distant hills, which were bluish, pinkish in tone; the middleground included the valley and the city of Addis Ababa. I indicated the houses with short horizontal strokes of white, gray, yellow, light ocher. Then I came closer to the hilltop where I was working: the bushes and trees. I used only soft pastels, first in a few strokes, then rubbing them into the support, trying to use the right shade, so as to avoid the necessity of too much mixing and rubbing, thus damaging the texture of the velour board.

Ralph Fabri

Final stage. HILLS OF ADDIS ABABA. The finishing consisted of more definition in nearby foliage, the completion of the solitary tree in the foreground; a few rocks, the shadows in the foreground. This being a cloudy day, the shadows and lights weren't very sharp, but they were noticeable and added to the picturesque effect. I sprayed the picture with a workable fixative, and added more finishing touches. Some of the foliage is done in meandering lines to give it a lacy appearance. At the end, I sprayed the picture several times, at intervals of about five minutes, and attached a sheet of plastic over it for protection until I have a chance to frame it under glass.

Step one. The charcoal layout is similar to any realistic layout, except for considerable simplification. As always, I went over it with yellow ocher and wiped the charcoal off.

Step two. I applied colors in very wet washes. This was necessary on the rough board, as I wanted to achieve an over-all pattern of lights and darks as fast as possible.

Step three. Although I kept the forms simple, they're all based on reality: modern balconied houses, big, colorful awnings, stalls and umbrellas of the European market, a suggestion of people, a couple of trees.

Final stage. MARKET IN DAKAR. Sharper forms, broken into a design which still retains the architectonic elements in the buildings. Trees, umbrellas, figures are highly simplified, but anyone can recognize them after a moment's observation. This is a true abstraction, in which forms and colors are reduced to basic features, even though contrasts are stronger than in reality.

Step one. I drew the outlines in every detail in waterproof black, sharp-pointed felt brush pen, over a light pencil layout. The felt brush lines dry instantly and I erased the pencil lines.

Final stage. CORNER OF HONG KONG. Working with a dozen colors, I applied light hues first, ocher, orange, yellow, gray, light green, light blue, with the sides of the nibs, to obtain wider strokes. I used felt brush pens with bigger nibs for the larger, darker sections. I made the Chinese signs look Chinese, but actually illegible, in order to avoid the possibility of painting a sign with some rather odd meaning. I did the figures and the car, but didn't touch the sky because even the lightest blue I had was too dark.

Felt brush colors do not mix as easily and correctly as other media. You can make a light hue darker, but the reverse is not always possible. Thus, you have to apply colors with some care. Washable felt brush colors mix better when you go over them with a wet brush. By and large, this is a medium for striking designs and colors.

One cannot explain often enough that final varnishing on an oil painting must not be done for at least a year, and preferably no sooner than two years after the painting is finished. The reason is that the aim of the final varnish is to form a protective, and removable film over the picture. If the varnish is applied before the picture is dry, paints and varnish become mixed up and some of this paint will come off, too, when the varnish is removed, thus ruining the painting. Varnish brushed over a completely dry painting may be removed without damaging the picture.

There are new, synthetic varnishes, which seem to be clearer, absolutely colorless, but make sure the synthetic varnish you buy is for oil painting. When I varnish a painting, I paste a label on the back, stating the date and the kind of varnish I employed. This saves any expert a lot of trouble when he tries to clean a painting of mine, because he'll know what solvent to use. This is a thoughtful gesture towards a total stranger, who may not even be born until years from now, and who will greatly appreciate this information.

How to do an outdoor subject in oils

On the following pages, I am going to give a step-by-step demonstration of painting an outdoor subject in oils. The subject I've selected needn't be done in this medium; it might just as well be executed in watercolor, polymer, casein, or pastel. My only aim in all my demonstrations is to show the technical approach in each medium, and to give you as much professional advice as possible.

Preliminary pencil sketch for the oil painting, Casablanca Crowd.

Oil painting demonstration (see color section)

For this demonstration, I selected sketches I made in the so-called Medina section of Casablanca, Morocco's great seaport. This old or inner city of the Muslims is much more picturesque than the European parts of the city. White houses, built like boxes, with blue or green shutters and doors, are contrasted with the blue sky and the brilliantly colored awnings. Crowds, dressed in Muslim or European garments, fill the intricate pattern of streets all day long. I worked on an even-textured canvas, 22″ x 28″ in size. Turn to the color section for illustrations of this step-by-step demonstration. I gave my painting the title, *Casablanca Crowd*.

Step one

On the basis of a satisfactory pencil sketch, I laid out the scene on the canvas in light charcoal lines. I went over these with a thin yellow ocher outline, and wiped off the charcoal. By the way, I measured the main vertical walls of buildings from the left or right edge of the canvas, to make sure they'd be really vertical. Nothing is more distressing than to see a cityscape in which buildings appear to be ready to fall over.

Step two

As in all outdoor paintings, I began with the background—the sky—and finished it before anything else, but only around the houses, going into the buildings with the sky, in order to avoid having empty canvas spots. The bottom of the sky is much lighter than the top, as usual. I mixed white with a small amount of phthalo blue to obtain the bright North African sky color. I laid out all other major colors, white and shady sides of buildings, working all over the canvas, jumping from one section to the other. I indicated the walls in different tones of gray, and added a touch of yellow to the white sides.

Yellow, orange, green, red, and other awnings came quickly, and the shadows underneath them, with only a few strokes suggesting figures. What I wanted was an over-all effect, because no color has any artistic meaning by itself. You have to compare one color with its neighbors before you are satisfied that the shade is right. Few, if any of the colors are just as they came from the tubes. This isn't a poster, in which loud, pure colors have to be employed. I mixed orange with burnt sienna, alizarin crimson with cobalt blue, and so forth, to obtain shades I needed. The shadows on the houses are white mixed with a touch of ivory black, ultramarine blue, alizarin crimson, and a bit of yellow ocher.

The dark shadows under the awnings are mostly ultramarine blue mixed with alizarin crimson and also with a little chromium oxide green and black.

Step three

Continuing the sky all the way to the top, I used plenty of paint. A thin application of paint in oils is not recommended. Varnishing, necessary in this medium, brings out any little dirt mark that might have been left underneath the color unless you apply paint in a solid manner. Most of this painting was done with pure paint, without any medium. I gave more definition to windows, walls, and awnings; indicated the street, almost covering up the figures.

Step four

Looking at my painting from a distance, I noticed that the walls were slanting to the left, despite my original precaution. I straightened them out by changing an illuminated wall here, a wall in the shade there. I also rendered the reflections of white walls and roofs in the shadows, then added the absolutely necessary details to windows and shutters. A window isn't a little paint on a wall; it's an architectural feature, with depth, lights, and shadows.

The awnings are also real forms, with shadows and lights, some plain, others striped, some in the sun, others in the shade. The shadow on an orange awning isn't the same as the shadow on green or yellow. Yet, you can tell a green or red object even in the shade.

I did the figures at the end, from good sketches, merely suggesting crowds, with a few figures nearby on a larger scale, but none with eyes, eyebrows, nostrils, and other tiny details. I paid attention to the mixture of garbs, the existence of the red fez, white and blue turbans, some western hats and caps. I made most of the shadows on the houses lighter, because they turned out to be too dark, compared with the bright white walls, especially in the distance.

My signature meant that I considered the picture finished. It's a realistic, but far from photographic work. Anyone familiar with North African cities is bound to recognize it. The square minaret is typical of the North African countries formerly under Spanish or French rule. In Libya and Egypt, most minarets are roundish, with pointed tops, and with balconies from which the muezzin calls the faithful to prayer. This reminds me of an artist who spent half a year in Istanbul and painted many pictures supposedly of that beautiful city. But she thought that those pointed towers were just decorations and painted one next to almost every house. Actually, a minaret has to be connected with a mosque.

Moonlight Sonata, watercolor on paper. The inspiration came from Beethoven's composition of the same title, but I placed the full moon over Manhattan, and tried to give the picture a dream-like quality. In a dream, images are interwoven in strange patterns. I applied watercolor in truly transparent washes, gradually, so as to achieve softness. Collection, Mr. and Mrs. Harry Hersch, New York.

15 Painting outdoors in watercolor

WATERCOLOR IS PROBABLY the oldest painting medium, but it wasn't introduced as a medium for individual paintings until the eighteenth century, when English artists began using it in full-fledged pictures, not merely in preliminary sketches and in topographical renderings. This kind of watercolor is now called aquarelle or transparent watercolor, to differentiate it from opaque watermedia.

Equipment for outdoors

For painting outdoors in watercolor, you'll need an enamel folding box consisting of a palette, attached to a section made to hold a sufficient number of colors. These colors come in cakes, pans, or tubes. For small paintings, pans or cakes are practical; for larger pictures, paint squeezed from tubes spreads faster. Water makes dried-out tube colors usable indefinitely. You need water and cans. There's a container-cup combination; the cup can be attached to the paintbox, but you need more water than such a gadget can hold.

Not just any water

The water used in aquarelle should be clean and pure. Some artists work only with distilled water, or rainwater, because impurities and/or strong mineral content may affect the colors, and even the paper itself. So-called hard water doesn't dissolve watercolors as quickly as soft water does. In my estimation, however, any good drinking water will do for painting, but avoid rusty, stale, contaminated water, and change the water frequently. You just cannot expect to obtain a bright yellow or pink with dirty water. I once knew an artist who, working in a small village, unable to find clean water, bought a bottle of white wine, and painted with it. (Most of the wine, however, was used internally.)

You have to sit

You cannot do a watercolor in a standing position because you have to hold the paintbox-palette in one hand, the brush in the other; you have to hold the support, too, probably in your lap. A stool is necessary, unless you know there's a bench or rock on which you can sit, keeping the can of water on the ground. Even if you know how to sit on your legs crossed in the Oriental fashion, the chances are that you cannot handle your paper and brush with the necessary freedom. Such a position is also bound to stiffen your whole body after a while.

Supports for aquarelle

Paper is the traditional support for aquarelle in the Western world. Far Eastern artists often work on silk. Ranging from cheap, machine-made woodpulp paper to handmade pure ragpaper, and fine illustration or multimedia boards, paper is classified according to weight and surface. Weight is measured by reams of 500 sheets. 72-pound-paper, the lightest we recommend for watercolor, means that 500 sheets weigh 72 pounds. The heaviest and best paper weighs 300 pounds. The actual weight of this paper, by sheets of about 22″ x 28″, is about ten ounces each. Boards are available in sizes from about 22″ x 30″ to 40″ x 60″.

Stretching paper

Lightweight sheets have to be pasted down on a solid board; we call this stretching. Wet the sheet and glue it down all round with 2″ wide gummed paper, half of it on the paper, half of it on the board. Scotch tape won't hold the paper. Another method is to bend the paper up all round, in a width of ½″; wet the paper, apply a fast-drying glue to the bent-up edges, and paste these down, pulling the paper outward all round while pasting it, in order to make it as taut as possible. European artists often glue their watercolor paper on the kind of stretchers we use for canvas in oil painting. In either case, the purpose is to make the watercolor painting dry flat, rather than in a wavy, buckled manner.

Pasted-down paper comes in so-called blocks, in sizes from 9″ x 12″ to about 18″ x 24″. These blocks are handy for outdoor work as they need no preparation. When a picture is finished and dry, remove the sheet by inserting a palette knife or letter opener in the short open section on one of the long sides of the block. Cut the sheet off by gliding the knife all round, with care. The next sheet is then ready for painting.

Hot and cold paper?

Smooth watercolor paper or board is called hot pressed (H.P.); rough paper is called cold pressed (C.P.); very rough paper is marked R. Recently, a medium rough designation has been introduced (M.R.). The texture should depend upon your subject and style. Probably most aquarellists like the rough or medium rough surface which gives the painting a certain sparkle, as the paint leaves many small teeth white. Beware of working on a very cheap paper with a strong grilled texture resembling a chocolate wafer. Such paper causes everything painted on it to look as if it had been done on a wafer.

Oriental paper, generally, though erroneously, called rice paper, with various degrees of roughness, has become very popular among laymen as well as artists. This kind of paper requires experimentation, and the right kind of subjects, in which the curly grains are not disturbing. A new, synthetic paper simulating this Oriental "rice paper" is now available. This synthetic paper, made of fiberglas, is fire resistant and quite strong.

Recommended list of colors

Alizarin crimson	Yellow ocher	Chromium oxide green
Geranium lake	Ultramarine blue	Violet
Cadmium red deep	Cobalt blue	Raw sienna
Cadmium orange	Phthalo blue	Burnt sienna
Cadmium yellow light	Viridian green	Venetian (Indian) red
Cadmium yellow medium	Phthalo green	Payne's gray
Gamboge (Indian) yellow	Hooker's green	Ivory black

There are other colors you might want to buy. Manufacturers have special colors, with their own names. Since watercolors are much lighter in weight than other media, a few more paints won't make any difference. White is taboo for most aquarellists. If you want to work with it, make sure to get the finest Chinese white which doesn't darken or change color.

Brushes

Work only with brushes specifically made for watercolor, and only quality brands. Round, pointed red sable, made of red kolinsky tails, is the best. You need the largest, No. 12, which holds plenty of water, yet comes to the finest point. A couple of small round, pointed brushes are good for details which require less water. Most aquarellists like to have a flat, 1″ brush for applying big washes. The sharp edge of this brush comes in handy when straight shapes have to be painted. Watercolor brushes have short handles because you work leaning over the support, not on an upright easel, as in oils. There are brushes with beveled handletips for scraping colors.

Before you buy a watercolor brush, test it in the store. They always have a jar of water for this purpose at the brush counter. Dip the brush into water, shake it out a couple of times; if the point or flat edge is sharp and straight, the brush is all right.

Pencil, eraser, other accessories

Use only pencil for laying out watercolor: HB or 2B (No. 2 or No. 3, in cheaper pencils). Have on hand a soft rubber eraser or a so-called kneaded eraser, but don't rub this latter kind too hard, as it may leave a spot on the paper which shows up in the finished painting. Get a natural sponge, or an artificial sponge with small pores, for washing out mistakes, and for removing excess water from your brushes without wearing down the brushes. White blotting paper also comes in handy. Rags are essential at all times.

Layout for aquarelle

Boldness is a great quality, but aquarelle is difficult to change. Start with a good layout, so that you won't find it necessary to abandon a totally spoiled sheet after hours of labor. Work in light, sketchy lines, and apply light washes, gradually developing the entire composition. Once the main forms are established, let the watercolor dry and erase the pencil lines. The eraser eliminates the pencil lines without damaging the watercolor washes.

Apply one wash after another. You'll learn that certain colors are very transparent, especially the dark ones, while others, such as cadmium colors, are remarkably opaque when applied with very little water. Every color is stronger if you use less water. The great charm of aquarelle lies in its transparent quality, so try to avoid the use of these colors in an opaque consistency.

White is the color of the paper

In true aquarelle, the white of the paper serves for all white sections. Make colors lighter by adding more water or by acquiring lighter shades of the same hues. The trick in this medium is how to go over one wash with another, and still another, without picking up the previous layers, and without destroying the texture of the paper. Of course, you can never go over blue with yellow, or vice-versa, without turning it green; nor can you paint a bright light green over red, gray, brown and other darkish colors, no matter how dry they may be. No watercolor is ever so dry as to enable you to change it by superimposing a light color from a different color-family, except cadmium yellow, orange and red, when used almost dry; and such opaque spots usually clash with the fresh appearance of the transparent sections.

Blending watercolors

Watercolors can only be blended while wet; experience is the only real teacher in this technique. You have to find out just how wet the colors must be for blending and drying without leaving a hard ring. When painting a larger surface, work away from another section, in every direction, and have a piece of blotting paper or a sponge ready to catch or pick up paint when necessary. It's better to start with a light wash and go over it several times. Many artists soak the paper thoroughly before beginning to paint, but I am not one of these bathtub aquarellists. I work with as much or as little water as I find necessary for each particular section of my picture.

A rainy scene may well be done by using a lot of water and dropping wet paint into it, here and there, allowing the paint to run all over. But most watercolors look better when painted with drier colors, under strict control. This is especially true for outdoor subjects. A cityscape in which nothing is straight, sharp or clearly defined may be all right if you call it *A View Through a Wet Windshield*. I always let my subject dictate the technique, instead of starting out with preconceived notions. In the final analysis, an aquarelle should look like a painting, not like a puddle of water into which someone had dropped paint, perhaps by sheer accident.

Maskoid or frisket

How is one to paint a bright, lively tree with autumn foliage against a blue or cloudy sky? How is one to paint any delicately colored, intricate object against a dark background? One cannot paint such bright colors over the dark ones; and one cannot possibly paint the bright, intricate objects first, then go round every tiny detail with the colors of the backdrop. Here's where a little trick should be revealed. Use frisket or maskoid, a substance related to rubber cement.

Make a careful layout, in every detail. Go over it with this substance, and let it dry. Paint the entire background over this: watercolor rolls off it. When the background is finished and dry, rub the substance off with your fingertips, and there's the white silhouette of the object; you can paint it any way you like. Maskoid or frisket may also be applied to painted sections if you have to change the background.

Maskoid: in order to paint light and bright objects surrounded by darker colors in aquarelle, use maskoid. Make a good drawing and cover it with this substance; let it dry; go over it with the complete background. Remove maskoid with your fingertips and you have the white of the paper on which you can now paint whatever colors you wish. Frisket is another substance for such blocking-out in aquarelle.

Changes and corrections

Small changes and corrections are possible in the early stages of an aquarelle done in light washes. You can scrub a spot with a stiff old brush or with the corner of a sponge. The entire painting may be washed off, if you're working on good-quality paper. Many artists like to wash their paintings after a while, because it's easier to work over the soft-hued picture left on the paper.

Some colleagues of mine paint out mistakes in casein or polymer white, let it dry, then paint over this as if it were the white paper. This is a clever idea, but one can usually detect the difference between the original paper and the place where white had been applied. Small mistakes in tones can be corrected by rubbing them with a hard eraser; others may be scratched out with a single-edge razor blade or an artist's sharp knife. Such erased or scratched-out spots, however, must not be touched with paint again because paint would come out dark and ragged over them. Never do any scraping before the picture is completely finished.

Impasto in aquarelle?

Watercolor cannot be applied in thick layers even if you squeeze the colors from tubes. The paint will crack off the first time someone hits the picture. It's possible to paint in aquarelle over polymer extender, no matter in what way the extender is applied. But creating impasto in aquarelle is, in my estimation, totally meaningless. An aquarelle ought to look like an aquarelle.

Varnishing watercolors?

There are synthetic varnishes for watercolor, but here, too, I object to the drastic change in the appearance of a true aquarelle by making it look different from what it really is. Many people dislike the fact that aquarelle has to be shown under glass and thus, it's often difficult to see, because the glass reflects the onlooker. I've been asked to varnish some watercolors of mine, and I did. First, I mounted the watercolor on high-quality board; then varnished it with polymer matte varnish which made the painting waterproof and gave it just a little sheen. Such a painting doesn't look like a watercolor, but the artistic value of the painting isn't changed by the varnish.

How long can you work outdoors?

If you want to paint a truly realistic watercolor, right on the spot, you're better off if you go out on two or three occasions, because watercolor painting outdoors is harder than you'd anticipate. The reason is that you have to sit and work in a cramped position, as wet watercolor cannot be done on an easel. You have to hold it in your lap. I suggest that you put things down, get up and stretch your legs and arms every half hour or so. Otherwise, you'll feel stiff all over. Simple sketches, of course, don't take long to do.

How to do an outdoor subject in watercolor

I am going to give a step-by-step demonstration on the following pages, but please remember that the subject I selected has nothing to do with the medium. Don't think that a seascape or any marine scene should be done in watercolor because the subject refers to water. Not at all. Winslow Homer has created great paintings of the sea in oils as well as in aquarelle.

Preliminary pencil sketch for the aquarelle, *Cape of Good Hope.*

Watercolor painting demonstration (see color section)

The Cape of Good Hope, where the Atlantic meets the Indian Ocean (but you cannot see a borderline), is a breath-taking spot. One can understand the name given it by the Portuguese navigators who discovered it. From the point where I stood, the promontory resembled the head of a huge beast, with its pointed mouth wide-open, ready to swallow anything in its path. On the left, steep rocks in horizontal layers; on the right, tapering down to the sea; on the near shore, rocks and small trees, with one cluster of taller trees; in the distance, the vast expanse of water meeting the slightly cloudy sky. I thought this view would make an unusual subject for my demonstration of watercolor. Please turn to the color section for step-by-step illustrations.

Step one

I had an interesting sketch, showing the zig-zag pattern of the promontory, as seen from a higher hill. Working on a 22″ x 29″ sheet of finest 300-pound rag paper, I made a pencil layout, measuring the horizon with a ruler, so as to make it perfectly straight and level. I indicated the shape of the terrain, the main rocks and vegetation. This heavy sheet of paper needed no pasting down.

Step two

I applied a light wash over sky and water with a 1″ flat sable brush. I carefully left the foamy parts of the sea round the promontory white. A few washes on the near part of the land sufficed to define the vegetation and rocks. As soon as the washes were dry, I eliminated the pencil marks with a soft rubber eraser. I don't like pencil lines to show through a finished watercolor.

Step three

The painting is a true aquarelle, built up entirely in transparent washes made stronger gradually. Orange, burnt sienna, yellow ocher, and cadmium red washes in the rocks; gray and alizarin crimson in the sky; light and dark green, and ocher washes over the right-hand section of the promontory; ultramarine blue, chromium oxide green washes for the ocean, with a light streak of alizarin crimson, here and there. I broke up the white foam around the rocks with blue-green ripples; indicated more and more of the land, the rocks, the trees, using various greens, sienna, Payne's gray. I used the brushes and colors wet, but never allowed the paint to run away.

Step four

The finishing touches depend upon the artist. How far does he want to go? I wanted to create a realistic picture, but not so that it would look like a photographic enlargement. I put more strength into the rocks by painting the cracks with a drier brush, especially at the base. I gave more solidity to the rocks on the mainland; indicated the waves near the shore and added a few rocks in the midst of the white foam; I also defined the trees, both in shapes and hues.

The cluster of taller trees in the left foreground came last. As all colors in this cluster happened to be darker than its neighboring hues, it was possible to paint them over the other colors by using more paint and less water. Had the cluster of trees and the foliage been lighter, I'd have used maskoid for blocking out this part of the composition.

Few artists can paint an aquarelle without making any mistake, and I am not among them. Fortunately, my mistakes were minor. All I had to do was to scrape out a few ripples in the sea round the individual small rocks. The heavy, rough paper permitted me to do this scraping with a corner of a single-edge razor blade. I just skimmed over the ridges of the paper. The painting gives a very good idea of the tip of South Africa.

16 Painting outdoors in casein

CASEIN, AS THE WORD IMPLIES, is connected with cheese—caseus in Latin, Käse in German, kasi in Old Saxon. It's a protein found in curdled milk, and has been used by cabinetmakers as a waterproof glue for many centuries. It became a binder for household paints in the 1930s; casein colors for artists were introduced a little later. Casein dries fast; applied with water, it's fairly waterproof, so that you can go over one color with any other color almost immediately. It was the first new painting medium for artists since the eighteenth century, and was hailed especially by those who were allergic to turpentine. Casein has only a very slight cheese odor, not a penetrating smell.

Equipment for outdoor painting

You'll need exactly what you have in oil painting, except that the only medium necessary for painting in casein is plenty of water, and a couple of cans for water.

Supports for casein

Casein can be applied to practically all absorbent surfaces, including non-oily canvas, but won't adhere to oily, shellacked, or other very glossy surfaces. Illustration or multimedia board, absorbent canvasboard are best for outdoor use. The texture of the support, rough or smooth, depends upon your taste and style.

Recommended list of colors

Alizarin crimson	Yellow ocher	Chromium oxide green
Cadmium red medium	Ultramarine blue	Cobalt violet
Cadmium orange	Cobalt blue	Burnt sienna
Cadmium yellow light	Phthalo blue	Ivory black
Cadmium yellow medium	Phthalo green	Titanium white

Brushes

The same kinds of brushes are used in casein as in oil painting, but casein is pretty hard on bristles and the recently introduced nylon brushes last longer. Work with nylon brushes in the larger sections; bristle brushes are sharper, easier to control, in smaller sections and details. Flat and round, pointed red sables are recommended for fine details and for your signature. In general, you'll want the same variation of sizes as you use in oil painting.

Houses of Hong Kong, casein painting on multimedia board 28″ x 22″. Due to the rapid growth of population, Hong Kong had to expand as fast as possible. Floors were added to old houses, often in a topsy-turvy way. Each floor is different. Signs, mostly Chinese, are all over the available walls; vast throngs literally flood the streets. I wanted to show the odd, overcrowded windows, awnings, and signs. The street scene normally includes men carrying big trays of food above their heads; jinrikishas (rickshaws) are still in evidence. This is no photographic rendering, but my response to a colorful, exotic city.

Medium

There's a liquid casein medium for use only when you work in a very wet aquarelle technique. Casein colors lose their adhesive power when thinned down to such washes unless you add a small quantity of this medium. Normally, it suffices to mix a few drops of it with the can of water in which you rinse your brushes. You might add a small drop to each color you're diluting. The adhesive power of casein medium is so great that you have to wipe the rim of the jar and the inside of the metal cap clean before replacing the cap after every use. Otherwise, you'll find it most difficult to unscrew the top again. Should the top stick, don't use a wrench, but hold the cap over a candle flame, turn it around a couple of times. Wrap a thick rag around the jar, just in case the heat cracks it.

Layout

A layout in charcoal is recommended, as in oils. Go over the charcoal with yellow ocher, or with any other neutral color, wipe off the charcoal, and start painting.

Applying colors in casein

Casein may be employed like transparent watercolor, with the tremendous difference that you can go over blue with yellow or red, without the danger of getting green or violet. You can also work in casein as if you were doing an oil painting, applying colors in full thickness, as they come from the tubes. And you may mix the two techniques. I usually begin with thin washes until I establish the main forms and colors. I continue with full-strength paints. Impasto, however, is impossible in casein. Thick paint will crack off within a very short time. What I do like is to apply thin washes over the casein, just as I use glazes in oil painting.

An alizarin crimson wash over cobalt blue gives a more beautiful violet than a mixture of the same two colors in full strength. Casein has a most fascinating dry appearance, similar to pastel.

Blending

The kind of soft blending done in oil painting isn't easy in casein because the paint dries too fast. Drying can be retarded by adding water, but this causes a muddy effect. Practice blending, if you want to have a very smooth effect. It can be done, especially on a rough support. You'd think a smooth support is better for a smooth finish, but just the contrary is true. And blending is most successful when done with rather dry paints brushed into each other.

Changes and corrections

Due to its rapid drying, casein can be easily changed, anytime. Just avoid piling on too much paint. In order to avoid the necessity of working on a change over and over again, get a piece of ordinary soft blackboard chalk, in any color, and use it for laying out the changes. Chalk is completely absorbed by the casein colors.

Casein dries lighter

One problem in casein is the fact that it dries lighter than it looks when painted. This might be all right in light hues, as you can always make them a shade darker than you'd want them to be. But what about dark colors? Black cannot be blacker than black, and dark blue can hardly be darker than dark blue. In order to obtain darker hues, add some alizarin crimson to any dark mixture, except red. To red, you'll have to add a little ultramarine blue. Strange as this may sound, black will look darker with alizarin crimson in it than without it.

One easy way to obtain dark hues is to spray the painting with a workable fixative, that is, a spray over which you may continue to work. Such sprays give depth to the dark colors without visibly affecting the light ones.

How long can you work on a casein?

You can work on a casein as long as you want to. These colors never become muddy, unless you use too much water, and they dry fast, so that you can make changes of any sort. You can work on a casein in a standing position, with the support on an easel, like an oil painting. This gives you more freedom of movement than aquarelle does.

Varnishing casein

Although casein is considered waterproof, it has to be framed under glass for protection against scratches and fly specks. I'd also worry about the possibility that someone might try to wipe it with a damp rag. A couple of layers of a good spray fixative help a little, but I prefer to apply a coat of matte polymer varnish, which gives full protection to the casein painting. Casein may be varnished as soon as it's dry. When you coat it with polymer varnish, though, you face a rather weird possibility, provided that the support is very rough. Occasionally, the polymer varnish settles in the deep spots of the texture and dries with the effect of a blizzard. This is fine, of course, if you like blizzards, but not otherwise.

Make sure to use just a little varnish and a lot of water, rubbing the solution all over the support as thinly as possible, rather than flooding the support with varnish. Watch for a half hour. If no snowflake effect develops, you're safe. If snowflakes show in the teeth of the support, grab a stiff bristle brush and scrub the varnish all over, with water, pushing the white spots out of the crevices.

Casein underpainting

The old masters used underpaintings in most of their works. Underpainting means that you do the entire picture in a simple manner, either in basic natural colors, or in monochrome—all in tones of gray or in tones of brown —and let it dry. You then go over the underpainting with glazes in oil colors. I find this a most exhilarating technique, but it requires experimentation and planning. A casein underpainting dries fast, but has to be separated from the oil glazes with a casein varnish. If you neglect to spray the casein with this varnish, you'll find that the casein absorbs oil colors the way blotting paper absorbs ink. Any casein painting can be glazed in oils, provided that it's painted on a strong enough support, such as canvasboard or multimedia board. Don't try it on thin watercolor paper.

How to do an outdoor painting in casein

The basic technical approach in casein is the same as in oils, with one exception. Since casein dries lighter than it looks when you first apply the colors, it's difficult to match colors in small spots. The change will always look different when it dries. You may have to paint over a whole section, in order to make the necessary little change. To give a more positive idea, let's say you drop a little paint or dirt on the sky, done in casein. You'll

Preliminary pencil sketch for the casein painting, *Villas Near Cape Town.*

probably have to repaint the whole sky in order to eliminate that little spot. Of course, you might cover it up with a flying bird, with the foliage of a nearby tree, or a cloud.

The step-by-step demonstration I am about to give you will point out some of the problems and the answers to them. The subject is by no means restricted to casein, nor is casein restricted to this particular subject or style. Other subjects would be executed in the same basic fashion in casein.

Casein painting demonstration (see color section)

The wealth of South Africa is manifested in the countless lovely private homes. One of the nicest suburbs of Cape Town, with its beautifully kept, spotless, but unpretentious houses, climbing from the seashore up a hillside, interspersed with tall and small trees, inspired me with its picturesque appearance. For step-by-step illustrations, please turn to the color section of this book.

Step one

As always, I made a satisfactory pencil sketch before starting to work on a 28″ x 22″ very rough multimedia board, coated with white gesso over pure rag paper. I laid out the composition in charcoal, went over this with a thin yellow ocher, and wiped off the charcoal with a rag. This wasn't easy on so rough a board.

Step two

I painted the sky completely, mostly with titanium white into which I mixed a little phthalo blue, less at the bottom, more and more towards the top of the support. I painted a few white clouds, softly, so they shouldn't look like pieces of white paper. I covered the outlines of the hills with the sky before painting the hills themselves, in very pale hues, especially the small corner of a distant hill on the left side. I also sketched the colors of the houses and roofs, but the sky had to be finished before painting the branches and foliage of the trees. Many students paint the trees first, then don't know what to do. One cannot go round each twig and leaf with the color of the sky. Well, here's the answer: disregard the trees. The lines of the branches will bleed through the sky sufficiently so that you can apply the dark colors of the trees as soon as the sky and the hills are done.

I added more details in the houses, and indicated the stone wall in front. I applied the casein quite wet, at first. This was inevitable on the rough support, but I worked on an easel, as if it were an oil painting, and never allowed the colors to run.

Step three

More branches, more details in houses, a more articulate depiction of the stone wall construction: spots of Payne's gray, burnt sienna, yellow ocher, bluish-gray, here and there, like chips of mosaics. I made the foliage in the background more complete in forms and hues. Even though I had no desire to give a photographic likeness, I did want to render the various architectural forms. Houses in Cape Town aren't mass-produced; every one of them is different, with a variety of roofs, chimneys and balconies or porches.

Step four

Final details in the small houses, mostly the blue one on the left, and a couple of other visible bungalows next to it. I completed the trees and the foliage. The trunks are in black, burnt sienna, a little ultramarine blue, with orange in the highlights. The dark sections of the foliage were painted first, chromium oxide green and phthalo green mixed with alizarin crimson and ultramarine blue; then the lighter parts of the foliage, in phthalo green mixed with yellow ocher and a touch of burnt sienna. Note that the foliage isn't like a huge piece of green velvet or a stack of hay. It looks like something growing out of the branches of the trees, a kind of natural lacework, through which birds can fly.

I gave the stone wall a couple of washes in ivory black, Payne's gray, and alizarin crimson, so that it now looks like a unified wall, not just pieces of stone tossed all over. I also painted the gate in the wall, the sidewalk, and the shadows on the ground. My signature proves that I considered the painting, *Villas Near Cape Town,* finished.

17 Painting outdoors in polymer

In polymer, the newest painting medium, pigments are mixed with synthetic, man-made binders. Polymer is accepted as the general term for these colors, but some manufacturers call their products acrylics, acrylic polymer, plastic co-polymer, and the like. Polymer dries almost instantly and is really waterproof, even though applied with water. Like casein, it may be applied in a completely transparent technique, but it may also be piled up in any thickness, in any textural technique. The colors don't change and the paint remains amazingly flexible. Roll it up, step on it, crumple it, unroll it, and you'll find no crack in the paint.

This quality makes it possible to store polymer paintings done on unstretched canvas or on any plastic sheet or other rollable support indefinitely, without damage to the painting, provided, of course, that the support itself isn't affected by the storage. It should be noted that oil paintings on canvas can be rolled up when new, but cannot be left in a rolled-up condition indefinitely. After a while, the oil paint will crack off. Old oil paintings are very brittle.

Oil polymer versus water polymer

Polymer paints are also made to be employed with turpentine and other oil painting mediums. Very few artists work with such oil-compatible polymer, as this differs from true oil paints largely by drying faster. In this chapter, we are dealing only with water-based polymer, which has great advantages over both regular watercolor and regular oil paints.

Equipment for outdoor painting

Polymer comes in larger tubes than oil and casein colors. Larger boxes are available, or you can place the polymer tubes in your old paintbox in a horizontal position. You need the same easel, stool, and accessories recommended for outdoor painting in oils. Instead of linseed oil and turpentine, you have to carry plenty of water and a couple of cans. If you drop polymer on your clothes, they'll have to be washed out immediately. Think of this, and wear something on which a few more spots of paint won't make any difference.

Supports

Polymer works on any surface, except an oily or greasy one. Manufacturers constantly warn users of this fact. Polymer comes off the support like thin film when you apply polymer to an oily canvas, or to an old oil painting, or on a wall previously coated with household oil colors. Follow directions, and you'll have no trouble.

A hard-backed support is better in outdoor work than one which tears easily. Multimedia or illustration board, woodpanel, absorbent canvasboard, heavy watercolor paper attached to a strong backing are equally good.

Recommended list of colors

The number of colors available in polymer is smaller than what you find in other media, but ample for obtaining any hue and shade. Certain natural pigments employed in other media seem to be allergic to the synthetic binders, so that synthetic pigments had to be invented. Many of the colors have the old, familiar names, but some are new. Look at the color charts of manufacturers to find out what such new names represent.

Crimson (and a name)	Ultramarine blue	Chromium oxide green
Cadmium red medium	Cobalt blue	Violet (and a name)
Cadmium orange	Phthalo blue	Burnt sienna
Cadmium yellow light	Phthalo green	Mars black
Cadmium yellow medium	Hooker's green	Titanium white

As in oils and casein, many artists like raw sienna, raw and burnt umber, but these colors can be mixed from the others. Why carry excess baggage outdoors?

Note: At first, polymer paints came in jars. Now, they come in roll-up metal tubes or in plastic tubes. There used to be discrepancies between the various synthetic binders, so that not all brands could be mixed with each other. Now, manufacturers have realized that intermixing of brands in polymer is as important as in oils. In order to be sure, try to mix polymer colors of different makes. If they mix smoothly, they're all right; if they curdle, don't mix them.

Since polymer dries very fast, never place more paint on your palette than you expect to use up within a half hour or so, but you can keep colors wet by adding drops of water. Don't forget to use a palette made for polymer: either a plastic palette with cover, or a very glossy paper palette. Try to keep air out of tubes by squeezing the paint all the way to the mouth, before replacing the cap.

Mediums in polymer

The best medium is water, and not too much, unless you want to achieve a transparent watercolor effect. There are two important mediums: matte and glossy. In some brands, both are final varnishes as well as mediums. In other brands, the mediums and varnishes are in separate jars or bottles. In some, the mediums come in tubes. In one brand, medium No. 1 modifies the consistency of the paints; medium No. 2 speeds the drying; medium No. 3 slows down the drying. Since polymer dries almost instantly, one wonders who'd want it to dry faster than that. A slowing-down medium may be helpful in blending.

Does all this sound confusing? It really isn't. You have to learn everything. Do you remember when, as a child, you first managed to tie your own shoelaces?

As in oils, use mediums sparingly. You can add a few drops of matte or glossy medium to the can of water in which you rinse your brushes; or a drop to each color, with an eye-dropper. The purpose is to make the painting uniformly matte or glossy. I prefer to use no medium at all, but I varnish my polymer painting as soon as it's finished.

Brushes

Use the same brushes in polymers as in oils and casein; nylon brushes last longer than bristles. Brushes must be thoroughly rinsed, time after time, and washed in soap and lukewarm water as soon as possible. Don't allow the paint to dry in the brush while you're taking time out for a sandwich or a cup of coffee.

Layout

Although one color covers any other color in polymer immediately, and boldness is a "natural" in this medium, it's still better to make a layout than to risk the necessity of drastic changes. A simple layout in charcoal is all you need; go over this with a thinned down yellow ocher; wipe off the charcoal, and start painting as in oils or casein.

How to apply colors

Whether you're planning to achieve an aquarelle effect, or a heavy impasto, begin with thin washes. It's easier to work over such washes than over the clean support, especially when the support is rough. Most professional artists try to cover the entire support with colors as quickly as possible, not only because the white support is hard on the eyes, but because one can obtain a satisfactory idea of the picture only when the entire composition is at least vaguely visible.

Once this over-all picture is ready, go ahead and work according to your heart's desire. An aquarelle appearance can be easily maintained if you continue to apply wet washes, without using full-strength brush strokes. But, in this fast-drying, waterproof medium, it's easy to paint a dark sky and superimpose light, brilliant colors upon it.

In an oil technique, apply paint in full consistency, adding a drop of water only if the paint happens to be too sticky. Work in every direction, rather than in parallel strokes. I like to use polymer in tube consistency, but I add washes, too, and go over some washes with solid paint again.

Blending polymer colors

Blending in fast-drying paints requires skill. You can keep colors sufficiently wet by adding a little water; or you can achieve the effect of blending with soft drybrush strokes. In outdoor scenes, a little roughness makes your painting more dramatic, more spontaneous-looking. But you must practice working with paint that dries so rapidly.

Changes or corrections

Any change or correction in this medium is a cinch. Just go over the mistake with other colors and forms. Here, as in casein, though, I suggest that you lay out major changes in chalk, before applying paint. Chalk is absorbed by polymer paint without a trace.

Impasto and textures in polymer

You can pile up polymer as thickly as you wish, but don't do it at once. Apply paint gradually; give each application a few minutes to dry. Otherwise, the inside remains wet for a long time. People have a tendency to touch thick impasto, trying to find out if it's really that thick, or perhaps because thick paint appeals to the vandalistic instinct dormant in many people. Imagine someone touching your thick impasto and feeling that it's soft inside and can be pushed or punctured with a fingernail! You may think I am a pessimist . . . but I've had all kinds of experiences, and I know people just love to touch things.

Materials for impasto in polymer

Instead of piling up paint, you might employ one of three excellent substances: gel, extender or modeling paste, and gesso.

Gel is similar to the gel used in oils, but this is made for polymer. It transparentizes any color without weakening it. Black mixed with an equal amount of gel is just as black as it was before the mixing. The same is true for yellow, orange, and so forth. I usually paint my whole picture, and apply gel with a small painting knife. On a big tree trunk, gel can nicely simulate the bark. Stones, plants, roofs, doors, and other objects can also be enhanced with an application of gel.

It has been my experience that gel acquires the color of whatever it's applied upon, within a few hours. This doesn't mean that you needn't paint it, or that you couldn't change its color. Go over gel with the desired hues. Polymer gel dries fast and hard; once it's dry, you cannot remove it, without damaging the support.

Extender or modeling paste, as I described in Chapter 11, is now made either of marble dust or of asbestos. Apply it from the can, with whatever tool serves your purpose: brush, knife, toothbrush, a wooden drink-mixer. You can shape it any way you wish; build it up high, scratch it with an old comb; carve it with a knife when it begins to harden; make holes in it with a pencil point or brush handle; turn it into a spiral. Let it dry and paint it. You might also mix colors with the paste before applying it.

Gesso, also explained in Chapter 11, is similar to the extender, but it's made with a chalk base. Its real purpose is to make any textile more solid by giving it a coat or two of gesso. It gives woodpanels, Masonite, or a wall a pleasant surface for painting. Applied in thicker layers, gesso can be textured to suit your subject. In all these materials, please remember that you can apply oils, casein, or watercolor over polymer gel, extender, and gesso, but you must not try to apply polymer and other watermedia over oil gel or oil gesso.

How long can you work in polymer?

You can work in polymer as long as you wish. You can start and stop anytime, any number of times. Just don't forget to wash your brushes and hands in soap and water, whenever you stop for even a half hour.

Varnishing polymer paintings

There are two kinds of polymer varnish: matte and glossy. Matte varnish gives your painting a slight sheen; glossy varnish makes it very shiny, and is mostly for paintings exposed to the weather or to the possibility of man-handling. The varnish looks like thick buttermilk, and everyone becomes frightened when first using it. One can hardly believe that it's a transparent substance. But it is crystal clear when dry. It has to be constantly mixed with water, though, while you apply it over a painting flat on a table. Rub the varnish out in every direction, evenly. Eliminate air bubbles by sweeping the brush over the surface; pick up accumulations of varnish along the four edges of the support.

I mentioned in the chapter on casein painting that, on a rough support, the varnish may settle in the crevices and create the effect of a snowstorm. To prevent this, rub the varnish with more water on a rough support than on a smooth one. Should the snowflakes appear, push them out of the crevices with a stiff bristle brush immediately, with water. Before you first use polymer varnish, you ought to try it out on a picture done on the same kind of support. It pays to be careful with any new material.

How to do an outdoor painting in polymer

I'll give you a step-by-step demonstration of polymer painting on the next few pages. May I remind you that the subject I've selected is not the only one right for polymer painting. Any subject in the world may be done in polymer, but this particular subject might have required a more painstaking technique in other media. And, in general, a complex subject can be done faster in polymer because the colors dry so quickly that you needn't wait for one to dry before you paint something next to it.

Polymer painting demonstration (see color section)

One of the greatest beauty spots in the Western world, admired since ancient Roman times, is Taormina in Sicily. A view from the town is unforgettable. The Romans built a splendid theater up there, so that those who didn't like the performance, would still feel they'd had their money's worth by enjoying the panorama. I was somewhat frightened by the vastness of the view, and made many sketches in pencil, ballpoint, and felt brush before deciding to do a painting in polymer. Please turn to the color section of this book for step-by-step illustrations of my painting.

Preliminary pencil sketch for the polymer painting, *View of Taormina.*

Step one

There are so many houses on the hillside of Taormína that all one can do in a layout is the general effect, the placing of the hills and the vegetation in front. That's what I did in charcoal, on a 19″ x 32″ rough multimedia board. The unusual width enabled me to show more of the scenery than one could depict on a support of the usual shape, which is approximately three to four in the proportions of its short and long sides. I accentuated the tall, dark cypress trees so typical of Southern Italy and Sicily among the houses. As always, I went over the charcoal layout with yellow ocher outlines and wiped the charcoal off. I didn't draw each individual house, just suggested a few major items.

Step two

The sky came first, as in all outdoor paintings. I painted the cloudy sky down into the hills. The distant mountain was next, merely a couple of shades darker than the sky, in bluish-reddish tones. I painted slight variations so that the mountain shouldn't look like a piece of colored paper cut out and glued onto the support. The nearer hill on the right has more visible details, in darker shades: meadows, rocks, trees, bushes.

The houses are in many pastel shades: pink, yellow, ocher, green, blue, violet; also white, with some walls in the shade, and spots of trees in-between, or seemingly above houses. All these items are light in value. Even the shadows on houses are very pale in the distance.

Step three

I realized that my sky turned out to be too dark, especially near the contours of the mountain; I made it lighter by going over it with white and Payne's gray, wherever necessary. I added more detail to the mountain on the right, more colors, forms, roofs to the houses, gradually covering the whole support with paint. It was important to keep the faraway houses subdued in tone, especially on a cloudy day. I kept the foliage within a similar range of values: lighter, more bluish in the back, with stronger contrasts, more yellow ocherish in tone in front.

Step four

I added a few windows where I felt they would help the effect. The house on the right has more details as it's larger than all the others. A couple of alizarin crimson and cobalt blue washes helped in pulling the scene together, and pushed the distant houses farther back. Finally, I completed the trees and foliage in the foreground. Nowhere did I include small details which would detract from the over-all view.

There's a good, old advice: don't paint more than you can really see with your naked eye, from a considerable distance. Far-sighted people often insist they see leaves in trees two thousand feet away. Maybe they do, but I don't believe it. I think they see what they know is there. The fact is that in art, as in eating and drinking, a little less cannot be as bad as a little too much. I feel that in my *View of Taormina*, I've created a picture which isn't an exact replica of reality, but gives a very good idea of it.

18 Painting outdoors in pastel

PASTEL STICKS HAVE BEEN USED BY MANY NOTED ARTISTS during the past three hundred years. The absolute permanence of hues in high-quality pastels should inspire more artists. The soft, dry effect of pastel is so pleasing that many painters work in casein because a remarkably similar effect can be achieved in that medium. Several kinds of pastels are available.

1. The regular, cylindrical soft pastels.

2. Semi-hard or semi-soft pastels (they're the same), which come in so-called square sticks, prepared with a small amount of wax so that they don't smear your hands.

3. Pastel pencils: pastel sticks encased in wood.

4. Oil pastels which can be rubbed on, then washed over with turpentine to give the effect of a painting.

New kinds may be marketed in the future. Ask your art supply store for folders on such pastels.

Equipment for outdoor work

Semi-hard pastels are probably easier to handle outdoors than the soft ones. All kinds of pastels come in cardboard or wooden tray-boxes, so that you have easy access to every stick. Work on an easel or in a sitting position. Take a can of reworkable fixative with you even if you're only sketching. For carrying pastel pictures, have the kind of canvas-carrier made for oil paintings; or take a fairly heavy sheet of acetate which you attach over the pastel with plastic tape in the corners.

Supports

As a support, any paper or board with a velvety surface, a good toothy texture, such as charcoal (Ingres) paper, and some watercolor papers, will do for pastels. There are special papers and canvas for this medium. Sizes of paper range from about 18″ x 24″ to 40″ x 60″, the latter only in mounted boards. Colored supports are better than white ones. If you work on watercolor paper, give it a wash first. The wash may be of different colors, harmonizing with the main hues of the subject you're planning to paint in pastel. Actually, pastels have a remarkable covering power, so that you can apply the brightest yellow or red onto brown, purple, or black paper.

The color of the paper ought to be a sort of intermediate tone, so that if some of it is left untouched by pastel, it shouldn't look out-of-place.

Squall in Kenya, pastel on velour paper 19¾″ x 25½″. I made many sketches in East and South Africa's National Parks. African scenery is often as flat as our prairies are, but always sun-scorched. There are clusters of trees, some very big and alive, but invariably surrounded by dead or dying shrubs and trees, which resemble prehistoric skeletons. A sudden squall in the distance adds a dramatic touch. I used soft pastels only in this picture.

Colors in pastel painting

There are some 360 colors in this medium. You don't need all of them in the same picture, but you shouldn't start without at least six dozen different sticks in soft pastels; you ought to have at least four dozen semi-hard pastels for outdoors. Indoors you need a larger number. My recommendation is that you carry about four dozen semi-hard sticks with you, and finish your pastel at home with many additional colors in soft pastel sticks.

Why so many colors?

The reason for the large number is that too much rubbing destroys the surface of the support, or weakens the texture, and the pastel powder won't stick. Theoretically, pastels are mixed like any other medium, but try to avoid more mixing than absolutely necessary. Apply colors directly, instead of using one color, then rubbing another color into that to make it right. Use pastel pencils or semi-hard pastels for finishing touches and hard, definite lines and forms.

Accessories in pastel painting

There are no mediums, but several additional items should be on hand. You should have some stumps (also called stomps)—cigar-shaped rolls of soft gray paper, with both ends pointed—or tortillons, similar to stumps, but pointed at one end only. These are for blending colors in small corners, or on larger sections, if you don't want to smudge your fingers. Paper tissues are helpful in rubbings.

Have an old bristle brush for scrubbing off a mistake. The rough brush doesn't smoothen the support, so that you can apply pastel over the scrubbed-out spot. Round and square pastel-holders enable you to use pastels to practically the last drop. They also help to keep your hand clean.

Layout

As in all media, a sketchy layout is advisable. Use any color, preferably one which goes with the subject you're about to do, but don't use charcoal or pencil. Pastel lines are easy to cover with any other color if you rub them into the paper. If you don't rub them, they'll be visible through the finished pastel picture. Don't leave lines where they don't belong.

Applying colors

As I mentioned before, try to apply the proper colors. For example, use a grayish-blue pastel for a gray-blue shadow, not blue pastel, into which you intend to rub black and white. There are several gray tones, besides shades of all colors, in a pastel set. Concentrate on main forms and colors. Use small amounts of pastel, just a short stroke, then rub it into the support. Experiment in order to find out just how much pastel you need for covering a certain space. The less pastel you use the better.

Changes and corrections in pastel

Colors are much easier to change than you'd guess. Just blow off the surplus powder, and cover with the right colors. A change of form is more difficult. Remove excess powder by tapping the back of the support, in an upright position, where the change is to be made. Take the old bristle brush and use it like a broom to brush more of the pastel off the paper. Never use an eraser! When the section is reasonably clean, apply the right colors. Another method is to spray the section, or the whole picture, with a reworkable spray. Do the spraying gently, a little at a time, but several times, until the pastel appears to be solidified. Touch it with a fingertip; if the pastel comes right off, spray it again. When it doesn't come off, you can continue to work on it.

Impasto and textures in pastels?

Can you obtain impasto and textures in pastel? Not at all. The whole concept of pastel would be destroyed, even if one might be able to manipulate some such effects in a tricky fashion. One might use polymer extender for an underpainting and give it a texture to take pastel. But what's the purpose of tricks? Let pastels look like pastels. That's what makes them beautiful.

Finishing a pastel

The final details are usually executed in semi-hard pastels or pastel pencils, which can be sharpened to a point. It's a good idea to spray the picture and see what the fixative does to it. Colors are often brightened by the spray, but they may lose some of their substance as the fixative absorbs part of the powder. As a rule, additional work is necessary after the spraying in order to bring back the original brilliance.

How long can you work on a pastel?

You ought to be able to do an outdoor subject in one sitting. There's no medium, no washing of brushes in this medium. The true finishing has to be done at home. Scrutinize your work on an easel and add the final touches in the comfort of your studio.

Varnishing pastels

There's no final varnish for pastels and even a pastel sprayed several times with a fixative is vulnerable. It can be scratched, fly specked; it can gather dust if not protected by glass or by an acetate sheet.

Framing a pastel

A double or triple thick mat should be placed between the picture and the glass. If the glass touches the pastel, it attracts pastel powder and this causes a kind of cloud through which the picture looks hazy, at best. Should this happen, remove the glass, clean it and put it back with care. The powder taken off the picture will hardly be missed. A pastel done with fine sticks, on high-quality paper, protected by glass will last as long as any painting and will retain its original colors.

How to do a pastel painting outdoors

The step-by-step demonstration on the following pages will give you a concrete idea of how I approach the pastel medium. I have to state again, though, that pastel is good for any subject, poetic or dramatic, soft or hard, mellow or powerful. My choice of subject in this particular demonstration has nothing to do with limitations in pastel. I might have chosen this subject for demonstrating oil painting, and my oil painting subject for demonstrating pastel. You can express your artistry and personality in one medium as well as in any other, except insofar as many people stick to one-and-the-same method, style and medium all their lives, due to habit.

Preliminary pencil sketch for the pastel painting, *Hills of Addis Ababa.*

Pastel painting demonstration (see color section)

The capital of Ethiopia, Addis Ababa, has magnificent natural surroundings which create the illusion of a temperate European, rather than tropical African climate. I decided to render a view of the sprawling city from the hills in pastel. This is supposedly a medium for delicate subjects, but I've found it satisfactory for any theme, especially where speed is necessary for catching a certain mood. It was a cloudy day, when distant hills practically blended into the sky; I could hardly tell where the earth ended and the clouds began. Yet, sunlight seeped through clouds or between clouds, illuminating the city. Please turn to the color section for the step-by-step illustrations of this medium.

Step one

Selecting a 22″ x 28″ mounted sheet of olive green velour paper, I laid out hills, valley, the nearby trees and bushes as I saw them, but pulled into the picture a solitary tree from about half a mile from the spot where I was standing. I drew the main outlines in yellow and ocher, and sketched the lower part of the sky in white and pale blue, in order to establish the composition. As I pointed out before, lines drawn in pastel show through superimposed layers of pastel, but rubbed-in spots are quickly obliterated with other rubbed-in sections.

Step two

I practically finished the whole sky with clouds, did the mountains and hills, the middleground, and began painting the bushes on the nearside. I also suggested the city with little white, gray, light yellow strokes. The original outlines of the big tree remained noticeable through all this. I went over these outlines with the brown-black colors of the tree. You have to apply a few strokes of the pastel, and rub them into the paper with your fingertips or a stump, or with a paper tissue rolled into a ball. Your fingertips, however, are the most sensitive and thus most reliable tools, except in very small corners, where stump or tortillon is needed.

I added rust, brown, gray, light orange, umber, and other colors to the olive green tone of the paper in the foreground and rubbed all strokes into the paper. More details in the background: bright blue, rubbed with a little pink, in the hills. I used white only in some parts of the clouds and rubbed even those into a light gray.

Step three

The branches and foliage of the single big tree constituted a significant part of my composition, and I did it in considerable detail. Details were needed in the smaller trees and bushes, too. I spent much time trying to render the reddish-grayish, uneven foreground, with the shadow of the big tree adding strength to this part of the picture. Due to the clouds, the cast shadow wasn't as strong as it would have been in bright sunlight, but it still remained noticeable. A few large and small rocks added interest to the space around the tree.

I sprayed the picture with a pastel fixative before applying the final touches. I made the upper left part of the sky a bright blue above the white-gray clouds, but the upper right-hand corner is practically the original color of the support. To give the foliage more depth, I went over it with zig-zagging, twirling lines of dark green and black, suggesting the lacy effect of leaves. I did the same with the nearby bushes and smaller trees. I sprayed the picture slightly three times, after having shaken the surplus powder off by tapping the bottom edge of the board against a table covered with newspaper. I covered the painting with a sheet of plastic for temporary protection. I feel I've caught the spirit of Addis Ababa as I saw and felt it. I call the picture *Hills of Addis Ababa*.

19 Painting outdoors in felt brush

A NUMBER OF YEARS AGO, someone introduced a felt brush pen with which shipping clerks could write names and addresses on any type of box or crate—paper, wood, metal, smooth or rough, in black, blue, or red. It was soon discovered that such pens worked equally well on glass, porcelain, plastic, concrete, or any other surface. A volatile solvent, with a nasty but quickly-evaporating smell, caused the ink to dry at once.

Layout artists began to use these pens, besides amateur artists who decorated porcelain and other objects with them. The pens were marketed under various names and brand names, such as felt marker, marking pen, Magic Marker, Flo-Master, Pentel, Pro-Jek, Zip, and others. More colors appeared, with a variety of felt tips: thin, medium, large, chisel-edged, round, pointed, square, T-shaped; some had big-barreled bodies with a large capacity of ink, others were as slim as fountain pens. Artists became intrigued and used these felt brush pens for sketching and drawing. Now, some markers have nylon tips, but they're still called felt brush pens. Why not? Aren't we talking about silverware when most of it is made of anything but silver?

Equipment

Felt brush pens come in about twenty-five colors, plus a series of warm, and a series of cool grays. These are for commercial artists, who use them in reproduction drawings, but some gray shades are excellent in fine arts sketching, too. The most convenient size for artists working outdoors is the fountain pen-type felt brush. These are marketed individually or in flat cardboard boxes easy to carry in your inside pocket or in your pocketbook. Get a sketchbook with a hard cover, and you can work even in a standing position. If you have a stool, it's that much easier.

Supports

For a support, you can use any paper, from bond (typewriter) paper and Bristol (drawing) paper to good watercolor or charcoal paper, in white or any light color. Illustration board is fine, too.

Recommended colors

Buy whatever color is available, including a couple of the grays I mentioned above; have some felt brush pens with pointed, some with wider tips. The names of colors vary. Some are recognizable, such as cadmium yellow, cadmium orange, yellow ocher, cadmium red, burnt sienna; others

Sicilian Town, felt brush wash drawing on artificial "rice paper" 9¼" x 13⅞". The outlines are in waterproof black, the washes were applied with washable felt brush and spread out with a wet watercolor brush. The paper, made of plastic ingredients, looks almost exactly like Chinese or Japanese so-called rice paper. It has a silken sheen which gives the drawing a sort of mother-of-pearl effect against the dark lines and washes. To make the street more interesting, I broke up the typical makeshift houses with strong shadows on the side walls, and under the balconies. I also emphasized the differences in the sizes and positions of windows and doors.

162

may or may not be understood by professional artists, such as aqua, sand, ice pink, peacock blue, forest green. They come in waterproof and in washable forms.

According to expert chemists, most of the felt brush colors are sufficiently permanent in what we call studio conditions. That is, if they aren't exposed to direct sunlight, and if they are done on good-quality paper. Black is said to be perfectly reliable, the blue and red hues may fade a little, but some of the colors are pretty bright, so that a slight amount of fading might be advantageous from an artistic viewpoint.

There's no medium, but some felt brushes can be refilled, others are thrown away when they're exhausted.

Layout

Since felt brush lines and spots cannot be erased, you ought to begin with a light line, preferably a pencil layout. Work with the lightest colors first, perhaps a light gray, before going into bolder lines and colors.

Techniques

This medium is basically for drawing; it's best to start with lines and apply colors with bigger tips, or by using the tip on its side, always working from light to dark because you cannot make a dark color lighter, but you can make a light section darker. The light colors mix to a certain extent. Light red over light blue gives you a violet; light yellow over light blue becomes green, but don't expect perfectly realistic colors and shades in a great variety.

Blending

The ink dries so fast that you cannot expect the sort of blending possible in any painting medium. You have to rely more on the optical illusion of the pointillists, who alternated yellow and blue spots, or blue and red spots, and achieved the effect of green, or violet, respectively. Like all new materials, this one requires experimentation, and that's what stimulates a true artist.

Changes and corrections

Changes and corrections with the felt brush are not easy. You can cover up an error with heavier lines and darker colors, but a delicate, unnoticeable change is really out of the question. You just have to avoid making bad mistakes.

Washes

If you're using washable felt brush pens, you can go over the lines with a wet watercolor brush and create a wash drawing. I suggest that you do the outlining in waterproof ink, black or gray, and use washable inks only in the coloring. The result may well be a nifty picture. On rough paper, the texture of which breaks up the felt brush strokes, the effect is even more sparkling.

Obverse or reverse?

On a thin paper, the felt brush lines show clearly on the other side, in a somewhat lighter tone, depending upon the quality of the support. Many artists prefer the lighter picture shown on the back, and plan their felt brush work with this in mind. In other words, they intend to show the reverse, not the original drawing, as the finished creation. This leads to certain complications. The picture on the back is reversed as if seen in a mirror. Such a reversal may be of no importance in most cases. A tree is just as good on the left as on the right.

But what about an inscription? Or a famous public edifice shown in reverse? How would it look if an artist made a felt brush drawing of Chartres Cathedral, with its two entirely different towers, and showed the picture on the back? Anyone familiar with that great architectural masterpiece would shake his head in disbelief at the towers being on the wrong sides. In such cases, draw the original in reverse, so it should come out right on the back of the paper. You can reverse a scene with the help of tracing paper, or by looking into a mirror.

How to do an outdoor subject in felt brush

This medium seems to be best for linear renditions; at least, a linear foundation. You could, of course, paint with felt brush strictly in colors, applied in the right shapes and sizes, without any outline drawing. The medium is certainly great for making on-the-spot sketches or finished drawings of architectural subjects, in which lines are often more important than colors, but colors enhance the beauty and the interest of the subject immeasurably. I am going to give a two-step demonstration of such a cityscape in felt brush. Nonetheless, I wish to emphasize that this is by no means the only subject for this medium, just as it isn't the only medium for such a subject; I've done sketches of seascapes and landscapes in felt brush.

Demonstration of painting in felt brush pen (see color section)

The older parts of Hong Kong have a dreamlike quality. One can hardly believe that such houses really exist. Almost every floor of every house is different, as they were added in recent years in order to give lodgings to the ever-increasing population. Streets are narrow, full of people. Chinese store signs cover practically every empty wall space between windows and floors. It's all picturesque, yet it has to be drawn with emphasis on the architectonic forms. You have to render the variety of patterns in windows, walls, store fronts, but without forgetting that those items constitute houses in which stores, restaurants, and people can exist as in any other city.

Step one

Working on a 15″ x 10″ illustration board, I made a pencil layout first, in order to play safe with perspective and proportions. As soon as I had the main lines, I began to work with a waterproof black, thin-pointed felt brush pen. Once the outlines were done, I erased the pencil marks and applied the darker spots with a wide-nibbed felt brush pen.

Chinese lettering

Lettering, in any language, should be done with a certain amount of diplomatic as well as artistic care. You don't want to advertise any particular restaurant, dancing place or jewelry store . . . or do you? In countries where the Latin alphabet is employed, artists suggest lettering by putting together letters which form no real word. The same method should be accepted in suggesting Greek, Chinese, Japanese, Hindu, and others letters or characters.

To a person unfamiliar with Latin letters, there's very little visual difference between E and F, M and N, R and P, but what a difference between Ear and Far, Moon and Noon, Rest and Pest! Imagine how horrible some mistakes in an unknown set of letters might be! Don't ever paint Chinese, Japanese, and other characters clearly, but incorrectly.

Step two

Please turn to the color section for the full-color illustration of this demonstration.

I had a packet of twelve different colors. I applied the lightest ones first: yellow, ocher, pink, gray, working with the flat sides of the nibs. I added green, red, blue, purple, brown. All the colors are quite strong. Subtle shades are not easy to obtain, but the bright hues are just right for an exotic scene of this sort. I didn't dare to touch the sky, though. I knew it would come out much too dark, without any contrast between sky and houses.

At no time did I expect to achieve anything more than a vivid, uninhibited picture. There are other media for subtle realism. Every medium should have its own place in your repertory of techniques. Utilize each to its fullest potential, rather than trying to make a painting look as if it were something else than what it really is. My *Corner of Hong Kong* in felt brush pen is quite different from similar subjects worked out in casein, polymer, or oil colors.

20 Abstraction in outdoor painting

ALTHOUGH WE FIND ABSTRACT ANIMAL AND HUMAN FIGURES in prehistoric art, and the art of all primitive tribes, as well as in children's toys, abstraction, as a form of the fine arts, is a recent development. Abstraction means that the artist reduces his work to what he considers a visually satisfying, and mentally understandable relationship of basic forms and colors, without bothering with perspective, proportions, and realistic details.

How did abstraction originate?

Early in the twentieth century, African sculpture was discovered, largely through the Anglo-Boer War, 1899–1902. African carvings served as an inspiration for artists who were eager to find new ways of expressing their esthetic concepts. After World War I, much experimentation took place especially in Germany, culminating in the Bauhaus Movement, which influenced every field of art and all the crafts. Functionalism, simplicity became the passwords of a new generation of artists and craftsmen.

Composition in abstraction

Although, at first glance, an abstraction may appear to be nothing but batches of paint, a serious abstraction needs as much planning as any other kind of art. Composition, the relationship between all parts of a work of art, is perhaps even more vital in an abstract painting than in a realistic one. In a recognizable work, nicely painted details may, at least momentarily, cause us to overlook a poor composition, a lack of originality or individuality. In an abstraction, there are no realistic features to detract your eyes from the total picture.

Techniques of abstraction

Make sketches as in realistic work, but concentrate on the larger masses. Put them together in what you consider the most artistic manner. Don't think that "anything goes" in such a painting. As a matter of fact, many abstractions are executed in a meticulous fashion. Generally speaking, there are two ways to start painting an abstraction:

1. Do a layout on the support, indicating only the main forms.

2. Draw the layout as completely as if you were about to paint a realistic work.

If you choose the simplified layout, apply paint in big masses, but not necessarily in flat tones. You may shade, blend or in any other way refine colors, if you wish. Some artists prefer to work with colors as if they were pasting on cutouts of colored paper; others like to create a feeling of three dimensional space. The important thing is to keep the pattern of the composition quite clear. Your colors may be realistic or arbitrary, or merely exaggerated suggestions of the real hues.

It isn't at all uncommon to see abstractions in which all important parts, such as houses, trees, fields, roads, figures, and so on, are easily detectable by anybody.

If you work on a fully-detailed layout, simplify the forms and colors as you're working. The end result is likely to be about the same as when you start with a simplified layout, but there are artists who find it easy to see the main forms only, while other artists can only see the details first, and have to decide for themselves when, and where to omit a detail.

Are you a "me-too" artist?

Certain artists or art students think modern art is the only kind the critics praise and the public purchases today, and they want to jump on the bandwagon, to show the world that they can do an abstraction as well as anyone else. These "me-too" artists are insincere in their work. You're an abstractionist or a realist by taste, training and habit. Don't force yourself to do something because you think it is the thing to do. Art shouldn't be a matter of fashion, but a matter of conviction.

Abstraction is helpful

One thing I must say is that abstraction teaches you how to see in big forms and colors, instead of getting lost in trivialities. Furthermore, how can you tell in what style and technique you could best express your own talent without trying out all, or most of them?

How to paint an abstraction

The demonstration on the following pages is based on sketches, experience and my own particular taste. Someone else would have done it differently, just as another artist would paint realistic scenes differently from the way I paint them. No subject is above or below abstraction. One can abstract a nude figure, big cities, small towns, animals, or articles. I may question the validity of abstract portraits . . . a portrait ought to be recognizable if it's to be called a portrait.

Demonstration of abstraction in polymer (see color section)

Sketches I made in Dakar, Senegal, lent themselves particularly well to abstract treatment because the mixture of native and European buildings, Christian and Muslim customs and garments is perhaps easier to suggest in a bold abstraction than in a realistic rendering, which might look like an enlarged picture postcard. Please turn to the color section of the book for step-by-step illustrations of this scene.

Preliminary pencil sketch for the abstract polymer painting, *Market in Dakar.*

Step one

After a pencil sketch of *Market in Dakar,* I laid out a typical street view of this African city, with the European market: stalls, umbrellas, tables, fruits, vegetables, housewares, and other merchandise, with people milling around. I used a 22″ x 28″ multimedia board. It was the usual layout in charcoal, over which I applied a thin yellow ocher outline in polymer. I decided to work in this medium because it dries instantly and enables the artist to make all kinds of changes without any difficulty.

Step two

At first, I used lots of water, but held the support in an upright position, on my easel. Running colors won't leave indelible streaks in polymer, as in aquarelle. The colors in this abstraction are stronger than in reality, but I never lost sight of the fact that the scene refers to modern, balconied houses, with some older structures in-between.

Step three

Here I added more forms, all simplified: trees, umbrellas, doors, figures, sharper definition of awnings. At this stage, I could easily have decided to turn my work into a realistic painting. Frankly, however, I enjoyed the boldness, the simplicity of forms. I might do another painting of the same subject in a realistic style, some other time.

Step four

I made the bright hues brighter, more yellow, more red, more green; added more depth to the darks: alizarin crimson over ivory black or ultramarine blue. Gradually, the aquarelle effect of the first layout disappeared under heavier applications of paint. The architectonic forms became stronger, and I gave the entire painting subtler shades by going over every section with transparent washes. I think the subject is recognizable to anyone looking at it for a minute or so.

Doing the same subject in different styles

I often do a subject in diverse media and styles, usually with slight changes in the composition. One of these groups I especially enjoyed doing was *Castle of Flemish Counts,* a twelfth century castle in excellent condition in Gent, Belgium. Gent is the Flemish name of Gand or Ghent. I made a realistic and detailed sketch on the spot, in ballpoint pen and pencil. The castle looked so beautiful that I added nothing of my own imagination to the sketch.

Later, I made a casein painting of the same castle, with small exaggerations in perspective, and adding three typical Flemish houses in the background on the right-hand side. Such houses are, of course, near the castle in reality, even though not in exactly that spot. I dramatized the shadows by making them a little darker.

A year or so later, I turned the theme into a semi-abstraction, eliminating converging lines and other features of perspective. I replaced them with an almost diagrammatic rendering of crenellated walls and towers. By overlapping these forms, and by painting them in richly varied yellowish tones against grayish shadows, above green-blue water on three sides of the castle, and under a dark, mysterious sky, I think I succeeded in creating a more personal picture. It's in casein, and the colors are applied so dryly that the picture resembles a pastel. I'm not at all sure it's the last word in this subject. I might try again, in a different medium, in a different style.

(Above left) Ballpoint and pencil drawing from life, shows all important details of this twelfth century castle in Belgium. Later, (above right) I used the same subject for a realistic painting in casein. I only changed the perspective of the structure to a small degree. The same subject (below) is highly simplified in this casein painting. I replaced converging lines of true perspective with overlapping forms, in which crenellated walls and turrets go over each other, as if they were made of glass. A three dimensional effect is achieved, however, by carefully devised dark and light hues in many subtle shades. The deep green-blue water and the equally deep blue-green sky with a few bright clouds lend the old castle a mood of mystery. *(Collection, Dr. Albert Soletsky)*

21 Finishing outdoor paintings at home

PAINTING OUTDOORS IS HEALTHFUL AND GREAT FUN, but not as comfortable as working indoors, where you aren't exposed to flies, mosquitoes, or sudden gusts of wind. It's also likely that any painting you do outdoors remains unfinished along the edges of the support, and some smudges or scratches are bound to occur, no matter what medium you employ and how careful you are. In more cases than not, you'll have to do the finishing touches at home.

What does finishing mean?

Depending upon your style of painting, a picture of yours is finished when it's on the level of execution to which you normally carry your paintings. It should be on that level all over the support, not only in one part, with the rest merely sketched in. As for your usual level of execution, you ought to ask yourself certain questions. Is that level actually right? Or is it the limit of your knowledge? Couldn't you, wouldn't you go further if you knew how? An experienced artist is the one who has enough self-criticism to help him give answers to his own questions.

Judging your own work

You can never judge your own work while you're doing it. You make mistakes of one sort or another, in composition, color, values, in perspective or proportions, without noticing them, because you're completely involved in your picture. But you can look at your painting with fresh eyes later, in a different environment. You'll probably discover errors in an outdoor painting as soon as you place it on an easel in your studio. And you'll find more mistakes (unless there aren't any) a few days later.

Another system practiced by well-trained art students as well as professional artists is to turn the painting upside-down. Strange as this may sound, you can see errors easier in that position than when you look at the picture right-side-up. Remember that a person practicing Yoga has a clearer view of the world by looking at it standing on his head. It's also a good custom to look at your painting in a mirror, or through a reducing lens. The psychology behind all these methods is that you see your work in circumstances different from the normal.

Don't throw early paintings away

Students often discard their paintings, usually by painting new ones over the old ones, with the remark that those pictures are worthless. They may be worthless from an artistic viewpoint, but they're valuable as criteria of progress. You needn't save every scrap of work, but keep at least a few early paintings for future reference. You'll see how much better you are than you used to be. Write the dates on those early paintings, too.

Manifestly, all this self-criticizing, scrutinizing can only be done at home. You also have a chance to compare sketches, photographs with the painting, and make corrections or even drastic changes in a leisurely fashion. More often than not, you'll probably find that you had put too much into your outdoor picture. Eliminate a tree or a rock, or a house; simplify a section in the distance; add more strength to an object in the foreground, and the painting will be greatly improved.

What about creativity?

While working on the spot, you are too close, literally, to your work, and are reluctant to make changes in what you see. At home, you can allow your creative instinct, your imagination to play a role in the finished painting. You can step back from your painting, look at it from a distance, with squinting eyes, make some changes, then stop and rest. Don't look at your picture for ten or fifteen minutes; take a coffee-break. Look suddenly at your painting again . . . and the chances are you'll discover something else you might alter.

What about laymen's opinions?

Laymen mean well when they tell you that they know nothing about art, they cannot draw a straight line (they invariably say that!), but they know what they like. The implication is that what they like is good, and what they don't like is bad. It's up to you to give, or not to give, lay friends a chance to express an opinion. If you do allow them to say what they think, listen carefully and politely.

But don't let yourself be destroyed by lay critics. Don't change your picture because a friend of yours told you to, unless you feel his comments happened to be right.

What about professional criticism?

Tastes are so different, and present-day art has so many "isms" that one serious critic derides the work another, equally serious, critic admires. How can you tell to which critic you ought to listen? I recall my student days. Most of my classmates dismissed the criticism of any instructor when the criticism was derogatory, with the remark: "What does the old fool know about art?" However, when the same "old fool" happened to praise their works, they invariably declared that "The old fool is carrying his brains with him today."

My attitude was different. I listened to the remarks of an instructor while he went around, criticizing the works of all my fellow-students. If I found that I agreed with the opinions of a certain instructor in reference to my classmates' works, I accepted his remarks and advice in reference to my own work without any hesitation. If I felt that his criticism was weak, capricious, illogical, or old-fashioned in general, I paid no attention to his criticism of my work, whether the criticism was enthusiastic or devastating. It just rolled off me, like water off an oilskin. May I suggest that you, too, decide whose criticism sounds right, and accept his criticism in connection with your own achievement, whether it's favorable or not.

Help yourself

I don't believe there's an artist in existence whose paintings have never been rejected by a jury and belittled by some critics. Sooner or later, though, a good artist finds his work accepted in more and more exhibitions. He'll win perhaps a very small award. He'll sell a painting—not to a rich friend, but to a total stranger. Every student of art hopes such things will happen. But don't just hope and pray. Do something about it: work hard, develop stronger self-criticism; visit art exhibitions; try to meet professional artists and watch them work.

Artists often complain that life is too hard for them. Life is hard for most people. Businessmen, white collar workers, men and women in all professional fields, have to fight for recognition, for success, and occasionally even for mere survival. Nobody denies the importance of luck, but what can you do even with the best possible luck, without talent or aptitude, without knowledge and common sense? Ultimately, God helps those who help themselves. Help yourself! Then, when luck comes, you'll know what to do with it.

Index

Edited by Susan E. Meyer
Designed by James Craig
Composed in ten point Century Expanded by Atlantic Linotype Co.
Color offset in Japan by Toppan Printing Co. Ltd.
Black and white offset by The Haddon Craftsmen, Inc.
Bound by The Haddon Craftsmen, Inc.